Redmine Plugin Extension and Development

Build stunning extensions quickly and efficiently by leveraging Redmine's plugin facilities

Alex Bevilacqua

BIRMINGHAM - MUMBAI

Redmine Plugin Extension and Development

First published: March 2014

Production Reference: 1120314

Published by Packt Publishing Ltd.
Livery Place
35 Livery Street
Birmingham B3 2PB, UK.

ISBN 978-1-78328-874-8

www.packtpub.com

Cover Image by Aniket Sawant (aniket_sawant_photography@hotmail.com)

Credits

Author
Alex Bevilacqua

Reviewers
Shamasis Bhattacharya
Petr Pospíšil
Kevin Vicrey
Mischa The Evil

Acquisition Editors
Akram Hussain
Neha Nagwekar

Content Development Editor
Larissa Pinto

Technical Editors
Aman Preet Singh
Nachiket Vartak

Copy Editors
Alisha Aranha
Brandt D'Mello
Adithi Shetty

Project Coordinator
Jomin Varghese

Proofreader
Maria Gould

Graphics
Ronak Dhruv

Indexer
Monica Ajmera Mehta

Production Coordinator
Alwin Roy

Cover Work
Alwin Roy

About the Author

Alex Bevilacqua is an advocate for open standards, as well as a passionate and enthusiastic open source developer with over 10 years of experience. He is skilled in Ruby, Python, C#, Flash, Flex, JavaScript, and others.

He is the author of a number of Redmine extensions and plugins; two of the most popular being the Redmine Knowledgebase and the Redmine Dropbox Attachments plugin.

He currently works for a leading digital marketing company in Toronto where he works on process automation, data collection, and aggregation initiatives. His personal blog can be found at `http://www.alexbevi.com`.

I'd like to start by thanking my wife Sara for being patient with me throughout this process (which should not have taken nearly as long as it did). I'd also like to thank Jomin, Larissa, and Neha (from Packt Publishing), and Misha, Kevin, Petr, and Shamasis (my expert reviewers) for helping shape the book into what you now hold in your hands.

Finally, a huge thanks to Jean-Philippe Lang, Eric Davis, Jean-Baptiste Barth, and the rest of the Redmine core development team for creating such a wonderfully extensible product.

About the Reviewers

Shamasis Bhattacharya has been a part of FusionCharts since 2008. As a JavaScript architect, he heads the JavaScript development team and spends most of his time analyzing, modeling, and coding the FusionCharts JavaScript charting library with attention to smart software design, continuous delivery, and innovative data visualization countenances.

He writes on his blog `http://www.shamasis.net/`, contributes to the community on GitHub at `http://github.com/shamasis`, and spends the rest of his time with his wife, Madhumita. He has also written the book *FusionCharts Beginner's Guide: The Official Guide for FusionCharts Suite, Packt Publishing*.

> Without my wife, Madhumita, tolerating my eccentricities, nothing would have been possible!

Petr Pospíšil is a very skilled programmer with more than 14 years of experience in commercial programming business. He has worked in banking, loan companies, and international companies with more than 7,000 employees worldwide. His experience in these companies was based on Microsoft technologies such as .NET and SQL servers.

For the last four years, Petr has been totally focused on developing Easy Redmine, working as the head of the department. Petr believes Easy Redmine to be the best project management tool thanks to its adaptability and an awesome team that contributes to the development of Easy Redmine. He has smoothly shifted from Microsoft technologies to Ruby, Ruby on Rails, and Redmine.

Petr coaches the development team, takes care of the quality of the Redmine core, and develops various useful plugins, not to mention his passion for rapidly increasing sales. He also likes cooking and eating good meals and trekking in the mountains with his cheerful fianceé.

Kevin Vicrey is a Web Development Engineer at Schneider Electric, in Montreal. He has over eight years of experience in front end and back end programming, using Redmine as the main project management tool. He holds a master's degree in Computer Science. He worked at IBM (Montpellier, France) and Schneider Electric (Boston, USA) as Lead Web Developer for five years. He has published many articles on the Internet about web technologies (`http://vickev.com`).

www.PacktPub.com

Support files, eBooks, discount offers and more

You might want to visit www.PacktPub.com for support files and downloads related to your book.

Did you know that Packt offers eBook versions of every book published, with PDF and ePub files available? You can upgrade to the eBook version at www.PacktPub.com and as a print book customer, you are entitled to a discount on the eBook copy. Get in touch with us at service@packtpub.com for more details.

At www.PacktPub.com, you can also read a collection of free technical articles, sign up for a range of free newsletters and receive exclusive discounts and offers on Packt books and eBooks.

http://PacktLib.PacktPub.com

Do you need instant solutions to your IT questions? PacktLib is Packt's online digital book library. Here, you can access, read and search across Packt's entire library of books.

Why Subscribe?

- Fully searchable across every book published by Packt
- Copy and paste, print and bookmark content
- On demand and accessible via web browser

Free Access for Packt account holders

If you have an account with Packt at www.PacktPub.com, you can use this to access PacktLib today and view nine entirely free books. Simply use your login credentials for immediate access.

Table of Contents

Preface

Imagine this: you stumble across a versatile open source project that outperforms most proprietary systems you've tested against, but it falls short due to just one simple yet critical missing feature. We've all been there before.

As hobbyists, developers, or just tinkerers, we dig into the code only to find that although the codebase is clean and well documented, we're not really sure where to start.

With Redmine, the answer to our dilemma is straightforward: write a plugin that fills this blank we've identified, allowing us to quickly implement *feature x* without having to hack the core system.

The Redmine authors have gone to great lengths to provide a plugin system that is extensive enough to allow even the most complex solutions to be quickly and efficiently implemented without having to resort to hacks.

This book will describe this plugin authorship process using an existing plugin that has been in production for a number of years as the basis for the various features we'll be implementing.

What this book covers

Chapter 1, *Introduction to Redmine Plugins*, provides an introduction to the basic structure of a Redmine plugin as well as some preliminary initialization and configuration settings.

Chapter 2, *Extending Redmine Using Hooks*, dives into how Redmine core components such as internal models, views, controllers, and helpers can be extended from within our plugin through the use of the hooks system.

Chapter 3, *Permissions and Security*, introduces the Redmine permissions system and how our plugin can make use of this existing infrastructure. It also includes a case study on how a custom access control system can be implemented by a plugin in order to limit access to content in a more granular fashion.

Chapter 4, *Attaching Files to Models*, highlights how quickly Redmine's built-in file attachment components can be added to our plugin models, views, and controllers.

Chapter 5, *Making Models Searchable*, walks the user through how some of Redmine's core plugins can be used to allow a plugin model's content to be included within the search system. It also covers how permissions are used to limit search results, and even how the default search functionality provided through Redmine's core plugin can be overridden, allowing us to further limit results using custom logic or permissions.

Chapter 6, *Interacting with the Activity Stream*, introduces another core Redmine plugin that allows us to inject custom events into a project's activity stream. It also covers how activity events are defined and formatted and how activity providers are configured and registered.

Chapter 7, *Managing Plugin Settings*, covers the definition and initialization of plugin settings and how a generic view partial can be provided to facilitate management of these settings values. It also discusses how these setting values can be applied within our plugin's views and controllers.

Chapter 8, *Testing Your Plugin*, provides an introduction to writing and running unit, integration, and functional tests that tie into Redmine's infrastructure. It also provides a brief note on how to integrate a GitHub hosted Redmine plugin with the Travis CI continuous integration service.

Appendix, *Releasing Your Plugin*, gives some pointers to plugin authors regarding what they can do to promote the release of their newly authored plugin. This is only meant to provide a handful of suggestions and not act as a de facto guide on plugin publication.

What you need for this book

In order to write plugins for Redmine, a working Ruby/Rails environment should be available, as well as a copy of Redmine.

Setting up Ruby is platform dependent, but we can get started relatively quickly. For instructions for Windows, visit `http://rubyinstaller.org/`. For OSX or Linux, visit either `http://rvm.io/` or `https://github.com/sstephenson/rbenv`.

The Redmine source code can be downloaded at `http://www.redmine.org` or from GitHub at `https://github.com/redmine/redmine`.

If you've never set up Redmine yourself, a comprehensive guide is available at `http://www.redmine.org/projects/redmine/wiki/RedmineInstall`.

Who this book is for

The target audience of this book is anyone who has basic to intermediate experience with Ruby and is comfortable working with Ruby on Rails applications. These are the basic skills required to get Redmine up and running in a local environment, which is where most plugin development would be done.

Readers who are interested in writing Redmine plugins and do not possess these basic development skills are encouraged to investigate further as there are many excellent resources available online. Some suggestions are as follows:

- `http://rubylearning.com/`
- `https://www.ruby-lang.org/en/documentation/quickstart/`
- `http://www.codecademy.com/tracks/ruby`
- `http://tryruby.org`

Conventions

In this book, you will find a number of styles of text that distinguish between different kinds of information. Here are some examples of these styles and an explanation of their meaning.

Code words in text are shown as follows: "Project module permissions are declared almost identically but are contained within a `project_module` block."

A block of code is set as follows:

```
permission :access_global_knowledgebase, {
  :knowledgebase => :index
}
```

When we wish to draw your attention to a particular part of a code block, the relevant lines or items are set in bold:

```
permission :access_global_knowledgebase, {
  :knowledgebase => :index
}
```

Any command-line input or output is written as follows:

```
permission(name, actions, options = {})
```

New terms and **important words** are shown in bold. Words that you see on the screen, in menus or dialog boxes for example, appear in the text like this: "If we were to check the roles editor now by navigating to **Administration | Roles and Permissions** and select any role to edit, this new permission would in fact appear under the **Project** category."

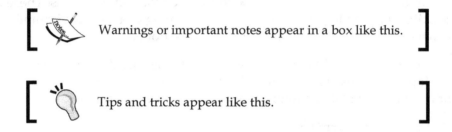

Warnings or important notes appear in a box like this.

Tips and tricks appear like this.

Reader feedback

Feedback from our readers is always welcome. Let us know what you think about this book—what you liked or may have disliked. Reader feedback is important for us to develop titles that you really get the most out of.

To send us general feedback, simply send an e-mail to feedback@packtpub.com and mention the book title via the subject of your message.

If there is a topic that you have expertise in and you are interested in either writing or contributing to a book, see our author guide on www.packtpub.com/authors.

Customer support

Now that you are the proud owner of a Packt book, we have a number of things to help you to get the most from your purchase.

Downloading the example code

This book continually references a sample plugin known as the Redmine Knowledgebase plugin.

This plugin is an actual production plugin that has been available since 2010 but has been continually refined by the author as well as multiple individual contributors.

The source code is MIT licensed and available at `https://github.com/alexbevi/redmine_knowledgebase`.

Errata

Although we have taken every care to ensure the accuracy of our content, mistakes do happen. If you find a mistake in one of our books—maybe a mistake in the text or the code—we would be grateful if you would report this to us. By doing so, you can save other readers from frustration and help us improve subsequent versions of this book. If you find any errata, please report them by visiting `http://www.packtpub.com/submit-errata`, selecting your book, clicking on the **errata submission form** link, and entering the details of your errata. Once your errata are verified, your submission will be accepted and the errata will be uploaded on our website or added to any list of existing errata, under the Errata section of that title. Any existing errata can be viewed by selecting your title from `http://www.packtpub.com/support`.

Piracy

Piracy of copyright material on the Internet is an ongoing problem across all media. At Packt, we take the protection of our copyright and licenses very seriously. If you come across any illegal copies of our works, in any form, on the Internet, please provide us with the location address or website name immediately so that we can pursue a remedy.

Please contact us at `copyright@packtpub.com` with a link to the suspected pirated material.

We appreciate your help in protecting our authors and our ability to bring you valuable content.

Questions

You can contact us at `questions@packtpub.com` if you are having a problem with any aspect of the book, and we will do our best to address it.

1
Introduction to Redmine Plugins

Redmine is an open source project management platform written in **Ruby** and built using the **Ruby on Rails** framework. It currently supports a lot of key features that a software project manager would find useful, such as an issue track, wiki, time tracking, source control management integration, and various other tools that assist with document and information management.

As the product has gotten more popular, the need to extend the basic functionality through the use of third-party plugins has grown. Redmine facilitates this through a plugin API that assists in hooking external model, view, and controller code into Redmine, as well as integrating with various system features.

This chapter will introduce you to Redmine's plugin structure, as well as how to generate a new plugin, and some preliminary initialization and configuration settings. We will generate a sample plugin that we'll be using throughout this book to illustrate various code samples and topics.

The following topics will be covered in this chapter:

- Basic plugin generation and layout
- A brief overview of the sample plugin that will be referenced throughout this book
- Overview of the initialization attributes
- Introduction to some helper functions that are available to plugin authors

An introduction to our sample plugin

Throughout this book, we'll be returning to a sample plugin, a knowledgebase, to provide additional insight into a topic, or to provide code samples. The plugin we're discussing has actually been developed over a number of years, and has numerous contributors.

For the purposes of this book and any future examples, our knowledgebase is a plugin that offers a hybrid solution that lies somewhere between Redmine's wiki and document functionality.

It allows us to create articles that can be stored within categories. Categories are stored in a hierarchical fashion, so a category "tree" can be presented to users on the knowledgebase landing page, as seen in the following screenshot:

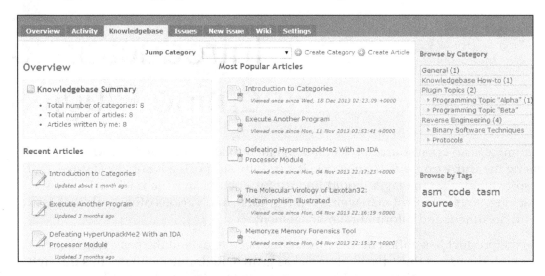

Generating a new plugin

Out of the box, Redmine provides a number of generators to facilitate the creation of plugins and plugin resources.

 The Redmine project website provides a plugin tutorial at `http://www.redmine.org/projects/redmine/wiki/Plugin_Tutorial`, which serves as a good starting point to quickly get started.

Running `rails generate` from the root of our Redmine installation will provide a list of available generators (truncated in the following snippet to list only those that are currently relevant):

```
$ rails generate
RedminePlugin:
  redmine_plugin
```

```
RedminePluginController:
  redmine_plugin_controller


RedminePluginModel:
  redmine_plugin_model
```

> **Downloading the example code**
>
> This book continually references a sample plugin known as the Redmine Knowledgebase plugin.
>
> The source code is available on GitHub at `https://github.com/alexbevi/redmine_knowledgebase` and is free to view, modify, and use.

For more information on these generators, the source is available at `/path/to/redmine/lib/generators`. For additional information about Ruby on Rails generators, see `http://guides.rubyonrails.org/generators.html`.

In order to create our knowledgebase plugin, we'll first run the `redmine_plugin` generator, which creates the bare minimum folder structure and files we'll need to get started. This is done as follows:

```
$ rails generate redmine_plugin redmine_knowledgebase
  create    plugins/redmine_knowledgebase/app
  create    plugins/redmine_knowledgebase/app/controllers
  create    plugins/redmine_knowledgebase/app/helpers
  create    plugins/redmine_knowledgebase/app/models
  create    plugins/redmine_knowledgebase/app/views
  create    plugins/redmine_knowledgebase/db/migrate
  create    plugins/redmine_knowledgebase/lib/tasks
  create    plugins/redmine_knowledgebase/assets/images
  create    plugins/redmine_knowledgebase/assets/javascripts
  create    plugins/redmine_knowledgebase/assets/stylesheets
  create    plugins/redmine_knowledgebase/config/locales
  create    plugins/redmine_knowledgebase/test
  create    plugins/redmine_knowledgebase/test/fixtures
  create    plugins/redmine_knowledgebase/test/unit
  create    plugins/redmine_knowledgebase/test/functional
  create    plugins/redmine_knowledgebase/test/integration
```

```
create    plugins/redmine_knowledgebase/README.rdoc
create    plugins/redmine_knowledgebase/init.rb
create    plugins/redmine_knowledgebase/config/routes.rb
create    plugins/redmine_knowledgebase/config/locales/en.yml
create    plugins/redmine_knowledgebase/test/test_helper.rb
```

As Redmine's plugin system is inspired by the **Rails Engines** plugin, they can also be considered as miniature applications that provide functionality to the host (Redmine) application.

Additional information regarding the Redmine plugin internals is available at `http://www.redmine.org/projects/redmine/wiki/Plugin_Internals`.

 When the plugin system was first introduced, Redmine plugins were effectively Rails Engines, but this is no longer the case (`http://www.redmine.org/issues/10813`).

The plugin skeleton that the Redmine plugin generator has produced includes placeholders for a number of features we'll want to include later, such as tests, initialization, documentation, MVC, database migrations, and localization.

Using custom gemsets in our plugin

As Redmine is a Ruby on Rails application, all external dependencies are managed using **Bundler**. This utility greatly simplifies dependency management, but by default only allows a single `Gemfile` to be evaluated when a bundle is being installed.

Although not provided by the default plugin generator, if our plugin will require external gemsets, we can add a `Gemfile` to our plugin root, which will be automatically merged by Redmine whenever Bundler commands are executed or dependencies are evaluated.

For example, we can create `Gemfile` in our plugin root directory as follows:

```
source 'https://rubygems.org'

gem 'redmine_acts_as_taggable_on', '~> 1.0'
gem 'ya2yaml'
```

When the Bundler installation command is run from the root of our Redmine installation, our plugin's custom gems will be included and installed:

```
$ bundle install
Using rake (10.1.1)
```

...

```
Using redmine_acts_as_taggable_on (1.0.0)
Using rmagick (2.13.2)
Using sqlite3 (1.3.8)
Using ya2yaml (0.31)
Using yard (0.8.7.3)
Your bundle is complete!
```

Generating models and controllers

The generators introduced previously include variants to generate a plugin's models and controllers.

One of the primary features of our knowledgebase plugin is the ability to manage categories. In order to implement this feature, we'll first have to generate the necessary model, migration, and controller code.

Redmine's plugin model generator parameters are the plugin name, the name of the model, then a list of attributes, and their data types:

```
$ rails generate redmine_plugin_model redmine_knowledgebase Category
  title:string description:text
  create   plugins/redmine_knowledgebase/app/models/category.rb
  create   plugins/redmine_knowledgebase/test/unit/category_test.rb
  create   plugins/redmine_knowledgebase/db/migrate
    /001_create_categories.rb
```

As we've provided some field details in our generator, the generated migration will be populated accordingly. The same process can be followed to generate the controller that coincides with our model.

Redmine's plugin controller generator follows the same pattern as the plugin model generator, but doesn't require field details:

```
$ rails generate redmine_plugin_controller redmine_knowledgebase
  Category
  create   plugins/redmine_knowledgebase/app/controllers/
    category_controller.rb
  create   plugins/redmine_knowledgebase/app/helpers/
    category_helper.rb
  create   plugins/redmine_knowledgebase/test/functional/
    category_controller_test.rb
```

Redmine's plugin views cannot be directly generated, but as they follow the standard Rails layout convention of extending `ActionController` and `ActionView` (http://guides.rubyonrails.org/layouts_and_rendering.html), we can quickly add view templates and partials to our plugin by placing the necessary files under /path/to/redmine/plugins/redmine_knowledgebase/app/views.

 Some of the naming conventions used by the plugin generators at the time of writing this book don't match the Ruby on Rails naming conventions. Database migrations should be prefixed with a timestamp, not an incremental value, and `category_controller` would become `categories_controller`.

The preceding examples were left intact as they reflect what the actual Redmine plugin generators produce.

Diving into the initialization file

Every Redmine plugin requires an initialization file (`init.rb`) to be included in order for the plugin to be registered with Redmine upon startup.

A stripped down version of the initialization file we'll be working on is included in the following snippet to highlight some of the attributes and helpers that are available:

```
Redmine::Plugin.register :redmine_knowledgebase do
  name          'Knowledgebase'
  author        'Alex Bevilacqua'
  author_url    'http://www.alexbevi.com'
  description   'a knowledgebase plugin for Redmine'
  url           'https://github.com/alexbevi/redmine_knowledgebase'
  version       ' 3.0.0'

  requires_redmine :version_or_higher => '2.0.0'

  settings :default => {
    :sort_category_tree => true,
    :show_category_totals => true,
    :summary_limit => 5,
    :disable_article_summaries => false
  }, :partial => 'settings/knowledgebase_settings'

  project_module :knowledgebase do
    permission :view_articles, {
```

```
      :knowledgebase => :index,
      :articles       => [:show, :tagged],
      :categories     => [:index, :show]
    }
    permission :create_articles, {
      :knowledgebase => :index,
      :articles       => [:show, :tagged, :new, :create, :preview],
      :categories     => [:index, :show]
    }
    # ...
  end
end
```

This plugin registration block contains field definitions that are used to identify the plugin to Redmine.

As of Redmine 2.3.3, based on the identifier with which the plugin was registered (:redmine_knowledebase in this case), the plugin would have to reside in /path/to/redmine/plugins/redmine_knowledgebase in order to be detected properly. Note that this can be overridden using a directory attribute in future versions of Redmine, as per http://www.redmine.org/issues/13927.

Plugin attributes

The values of these fields are used to either identify the plugin to the administrator when they visit the plugin list at http://localhost:3000/admin/plugins of their Redmine deployment, or to provide some assignment or initialization functionality.

Plugins

Knowledgebase
A plugin for Redmine that adds knowledgebase functionality   Alex Bevilacqua   2.3.0   Configure
https://github.com/alexbevi/redmine_knowledgebase

Ruby on Rails application default to port 3000 when run locally. As this is standard, we'll be using http://localhost:3000 as the base URL for all Redmine links.

The attributes that can be provided to the Redmine::Plugin.register block are as follows:

- name: This is the full name of the plugin.

- description: This gives a brief description of what the plugin does.

- `url`: This is the website of the plugin itself. This is generally the online repository URL (GitHub, Bitbucket, Google Code, and so on), or plugin website (if available or applicable).

- `author`: This holds the name(s) of the author(s) of the plugin.

- `author_url`: This is generally the link to either the author(s)' e-mail addresses or blogs.

- `version`: This is the internal version number of the plugin. Though not required, it is a good practice to use **Semantic Versioning** (see `http://semver.org` for more information), as Redmine follows a similar (though not official) numbering scheme.

- `settings`: This field is used to define and set the default values of internal plugin settings and link to a view partial, which system administrators can use to set plugin configuration values.

```
settings :default => {
    :sort_category_tree => true,
  }, :partial => 'settings/knowledgebase_settings'
```

The preceding example lets our plugin know that we will be providing a configuration partial, as well as initializing a custom settings value of `sort_category_tree` to `true`.

As Redmine plugins follow the standard Ruby on Rails application hierarchy, the implied location of our settings partial would be `/path/to/redmine/plugins/redmine_knowledgebase/app/views/settings/_knowledgebase_settings.html.erb`.

Settings management will be covered in more detail in *Chapter 7, Managing Plugin Settings*.

Initialization checks

Redmine provides a number of helper functions that can be used to assist plugin authors ensuring compatibility with different versions of Redmine, as well as other plugins.

Checking for a specific Redmine version

The version or versions of Redmine that a plugin is compatible with can be specified within the plugin initialization file using the `requires_redmine` helper.

This helper allows the plugin author to alert Redmine system administrators that the plugin is not intended to run with the administrator's version of Redmine. Some examples of the types of version checks that can be performed are as follows:

- Exact match

```
requires_redmine "2.3.3"
requires_redmine :version => "2.3.3"
```

- Exact match of more than one version

```
requires_redmine :version => ["2.2.0", "2.3.0"]
```

- Match a specific version and revision

```
requires_redmine "2.3"
requires_redmine :version => "2.3"
```

- Minimum version or higher

```
requires_redmine :version_or_higher => "2.3.3"
```

- Range of versions

```
requires_redmine :version => "2.2.0".."2.3.0"
requires_redmine :version => "2.2".."2.3"
```

Ensuring the existence of other plugins

Similar to the `requires_redmine` helper, the `requires_redmine_plugin` function is used to limit the successful deployment of our plugin based on the availability of another Redmine plugin.

The following examples are based on a plugin named `:sample_plugin` being included for availability and version checks:

- Exact match

```
requires_redmine_plugin :sample_plugin :version => "1.0.0"
requires_redmine_plugin :sample_plugin "1.0.0"
```

- Minimum version or higher

```
requires_redmine_plugin :sample_plugin :version_or_higher =>
"1.0.0"
```

- Range of versions

```
requires_redmine_plugin :sample_plugin :version => ["0.1.0",
"0.2.0"]
```

Extending core Redmine features

Now that we've initialized our plugin with some basic details and requirements, we can start integrating directly with Redmine.

A number of helper methods are available to plugin authors, which facilitate this integration with core components, such as menus and permissions.

Working with Redmine menus

The `menu` helper, which is also aliased to `add_menu_item`, allows us to inject custom entries into various content areas of Redmine. The syntax for adding a menu item is:

```
menu(menu, item, url, options = {})
```

The options hash can accept any number of the following parameters:

- `:param`: This is the parameter key that will be used as the project ID (the default is `:id`).
- `:if`: This is a proc that prevents the menu from rendering unless it is evaluated to true.
- `:caption`: This is the menu caption (label), which can be a localized symbol, proc, or string.
- `:before` or `:after`: This is used to position the menu entry relative to an existing entry. For example, `:after => :activity`, or `:before => :issues`.
- `:first` or `:last`: If either of these options is set to `true`, the menu item will be placed at the absolute beginning or end of the target menu.
- `:html`: This is a hash of HTML options that will be passed to the `link_to` instance that is used to render the menu item.

Redmine also provides a function we can use in our plugin to remove menu items, the syntax for which is:

```
delete_menu_item(menu, item)
```

The following example injects an entry into the project menu. Note that although you've added a new menu item, it may still not be available to all users due to insufficient permissions.

```
menu :project_menu,
  :articles,
  { :controller => 'articles', :action => 'index' },
  :caption => :knowledgebase_title,
```

```
:after => :activity,
:param => :project_id
```

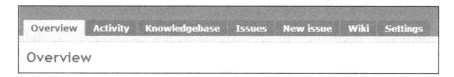

The other valid targets for the menu are `admin_menu`, `top_menu`, `account_menu`, and `application_menu`.

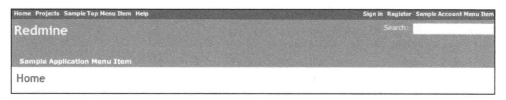

The `admin_menu` target is used to add custom entries to the **Administration** menu, which is available at `http://localhost:3000/admin`, and can insert custom entries between the **Settings** and **Plugins** menu items.

Initializing named permissions

The `permission` helper is used to define a named permission for the given actions. The syntax for this helper is:

```
permission(name, actions, options = {})
```

The actions argument is a hash with controllers as keys and actions as values (a single value or an array):

```
permission :destroy_contacts, { :contacts => :destroy }
permission :view_contacts,    { :contacts => [:index, :show] }
```

The valid options are as follows:

- `:public`: This changes the permission to public if set to `true` (implicitly given to any user)

- `:require`: This can be set to either `:loggedin` or `:member`, and is used to further restrict the types of users the permission can be applied to

- `:read`: This is set to `true` so that the permission is still granted on closed projects

Permissions will be covered in more detail in *Chapter 3, Permissions and Security*.

Project module availability

If our plugin will be adding functionality at the project level (as opposed to globally) within Redmine, we'll need to define a `project_module` block.

A project module is effectively a functional area within Redmine whose data belongs to a specific project, or whose scope can be limited to a project. Examples of project modules are issues, documents, wikis, or time tracking features.

Permissions defined within the `project_module` block will be bound to the module, as follows:

```
project_module :knowledgebase do
  permission :view_articles, {
    :knowledgebase => :index,
    :articles      => [:show, :tagged],
    :categories    => [:index, :show]
  }
  permission :comment_and_rate_articles, {
    :knowledgebase => :index,
    :articles      => [:show, :tagged, :rate, :comment, :add_comment],
    :categories    => [:index, :show]
  }
  # ...
end
```

Adding custom events to the activity stream

Activity providers are essentially models that have been defined to provide events to the activity fetcher. Once a model has registered an activity provider, activities will be mixed into a project's activity stream.

A model can provide several activity event types, which are registered by passing event types and optional class names to the `activity_provider` helper plugin:

```
activity_provider :news
activity_provider :scrums, :class_name => 'Meeting'
activity_provider :issues, :class_name => ['Issue', 'Journal']
```

Using the `activity_provider` helper simply indicates that there are activity providers registered. The syntax for the helper functions is:

```
activity_provider(*args)
```

The helper simply wraps `Redmine::Activity.register`, which is available at `/path/to/redmine/lib/redmine/activity.rb`.

A matching `acts_as_activity_provider` entity must be initialized at the model level in order to actually utilize this functionality.

We will cover activity provider configuration in more detail in *Chapter 6, Interacting with the Activity Stream.*

Registering custom text formatting macros

Our knowledgebase plugin will be used to create articles, which we may want to reference in other Redmine content areas.

For example, if we want to register the kb#1 macro to link to a knowledgebase article with an ID value of 1, we would first need to register the macro with a `Redmine::WikiFormatting::Macros.register` block similar to the following:

```
Redmine::WikiFormatting::Macros.register do
  desc "Knowledge base Article link Macro, using the kb# format"
  macro :kb do |obj, args|
    args, options = extract_macro_options(args, :parent)
    raise 'One argument expected' if args.size != 1
    article = KbArticle.find(args.first)
    link_to_article(article)
  end
end
```

We could now include the text kb#1 in an issue, document, wiki, or anywhere else where Redmine formats text (see http://www.redmine.org/projects/redmine/ wiki/RedmineTextFormatting for existing formatting options) and it would render as a link back to our knowledgebase article.

Summary

We now have a better understanding of what options are available to us when setting up a plugin for use with Redmine.

In this chapter, we covered the various plugin attributes that can be used to identify the plugin to Redmine. We also introduced some helper methods, which we'll be returning to throughout the book when we cover elements such as permissions, activity streams, and configuration in more detail.

In the next chapter, we will extend our knowledgebase plugin through the use of view hooks.

2
Extending Redmine Using Hooks

Redmine, at its core, is a project management and issue tracking system. Its developers have invested a lot of time and energy into building an extremely robust solution that rivals even proprietary competitors, but we occasionally find ourselves wishing we could perform a certain task or see a piece of information differently.

Thankfully, Redmine was designed with extensibility in mind. Not only is there a plugin system in place to allow custom functionality to be implemented, but core features can be extended using a system of hooks and callbacks.

In this chapter, we will dive into the various classifications of hooks and how our plugin can leverage them to add new functionality to existing Redmine systems and components.

We will cover the following topics in this chapter:

- An introduction to what a hook is
- What types of hooks exist and where they can be used
- An example view hook implementation

Understanding hooks

A hook is essentially just a listener for which we've registered a callback function. These callback functions expect a single parameter: a hash that provides some context to the function. The contents of the hash depend on what type of hook is being evaluated.

There are four basic categories of hooks available in Redmine:

- View hooks
- Controller hooks
- Model hooks
- Helper hooks

For view and controller hooks, the context hash contains the following fields as well as data specific to the hook being used:

- `:project`: This is the current project
- `:request`: This contains the current web request instance
- `:controller`: This contains the current controller instance
- `:hook_caller`: This holds the object that called the hook

 The full list of available hooks is maintained at `http://www.redmine.org/projects/redmine/wiki/Hooks_List`.

To quickly build the hook list for the version of Redmine you have installed, run the following commands:

```
cd /path/to/redmine/app
grep -r call_hook *
```

By doing this from the `app` directory, we prune out any results from the hook class definition or any of the test files.

Redmine has many hooks registered throughout the codebase by means of the `call_hook` method, whose syntax is as follows:

```
call_hook(hook, context={})
```

For example, the partial `/path/to/redmine/app/views/issues/_form.html.erb` contains the following hook declaration:

```
<%= call_hook(:view_issues_form_details_bottom, { :issue =>
  @issue, :form => f }) %>
```

View hooks

The primary use of hooks in Redmine is to inject functionality into an existing view.

A view hook is executed while the HTML code of a view is being rendered.

View hooks are likely to be the most frequently used type of hook by plugin authors. Through these hooks, we can add functionality from our plugins to existing Redmine views and partials.

As an example, let's add the ability to associate knowledgebase articles with an issue. We'll implement this in a similar fashion to how issues can be associated with each other.

In order to display this association, we will extend the relevant issue views using view hooks. To accomplish this, the first step is to create a class that extends Redmine::Hook::ViewListener:

```
module RedmineKnowledgebase
  class Hooks < Redmine::Hook::ViewListener
    render_on :view_issues_show_description_bottom,
              :partial => 'redmine_knowledgebase/hooks/view_issues_
show_description_bottom'
  end
end
```

This file will be saved to our plugin's lib folder as /path/to/redmine/plugins/ redmine_knowledgebase/lib/hooks.rb.

To include the custom hook in our plugin, the hooks.rb file will simply need to be added to the plugin's init.rb file as a requirement.

The preceding hook implementation is done using the render_on helper method, which facilitates rendering a partial using the context.

In the following sample, we'll accomplish the same result by defining the callback method ourselves and manually configuring the context object:

```
module RedmineKnowledgebase
  class Hooks < Redmine::Hook::ViewListener
    def view_issues_show_description_bottom(context = {})
      # the controller parameter is part of the current params object
      # This will render the partial into a string and return it.
      context[:controller].send(:render_to_string, {
        :partial => " redmine_knowledgebase/hooks/view_issues_show_
description_bottom",
        :locals => context
      })

      # Instead of the above statement, you could return any string
generated
```

```
            # by your code. That string will be included into the view
          end
        end
  end
```

When this hook is called and a callback has been registered, it will yield raw HTML code that will be inserted in the following issue form details:

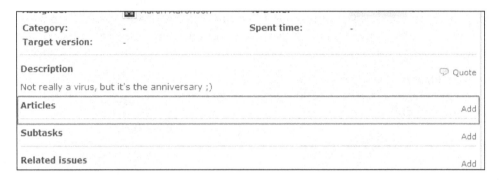

In our example, we've added an **Articles** section to the issues of the current project. Note that the actual implementation code for this is not covered as it goes a bit out of the scope of this book.

Controller hooks

Controller hooks allow custom functionality to be injected into an existing process. A normal use-case for this type of hook is to perform some custom validation on the context object provided to the callback.

In /path/to/redmine/app/models/issue.rb, there is a hook registered for controller_issues_edit_before_save. In order to take advantage of this hook, we would have to provide our own callback function. This can be done as follows:

```
module Knowledgebase
  module Hooks
    class ControllerIssuesEditBeforeSaveHook
      < Redmine::Hook::ViewListener
      def controller_issues_edit_before_save(context={})
        if context[:params] && context[:params][:issue]
          if User.current.allowed_to?(:assign_article_to_issue,
            context[:issue].project)
            if context[:params][:issue][:article_id].present?
              article = KbArticle.find_by_id(context[:params]
                [:issue][:article_id])
```

```
                    if article.category.project ==
                       context[:issue].project
                       context[:issue].article = article
                    end
                 else
                    context[:issue].article = nil
                 end
              end
           end
           return ''
        end
     end
   end
end
```

Once registered, this hook will check to see whether the current user has permission to attach a knowledgebase article to an issue before saving the issue.

Model hooks

These hooks are used even less frequently than controller hooks but are being included here for completeness.

Model extension is better handled through the use of new methods or encapsulation of existing methods by means of the alias_method_chain pattern. For a summary of alias_method_chain see http://stackoverflow.com/a/3697391.

A common use-case for model hooks is the :model_project_copy_before_save hook as this can be used to replicate content from our plugin that belonged to a specific project if that project is copied:

```
module RedmineKnowledgebase
  class Hooks < Redmine::Hook::ViewListener
    def model_project_copy_before_save(context = {})
      source = context[:source_project]
      destination = context[:destination_project]

      if source.module_enabled?(:redmine_knowledgebase)
        # TODO: clone all categories
        # TODO: clone all articles
        # TODO: ensure cloned articles refer to cloned categories
      end
    end
  end
end
```

The actual implementation has been left out in the preceding snippet, but placeholders have been left intact to illustrate what actions we could be taking.

Helper hooks

According to the official Redmine hooks list, there is only a single helper hook currently available (`http://www.redmine.org/projects/redmine/wiki/Hooks_List#Helper-hooks`). The `:helper_issues_show_details_after_setting` hook is called when journal details are being rendered in an issue and can be used to override the label and value that is passed to the journal entry.

A sample view hook implementation

We will be glossing over a lot of implementation details as they are out of the scope for this book, but the full code will be available on the GitHub repository at `https://github.com/alexbevi/redmine_knowledgebase`.

Identifying the callback

We've determined that our plugin will be hooking into the existing issue tracking system in order to allow users to attach knowledgebase articles.

The desired functionality is the same as the **Subtasks** functionality that already exists, so we will model our hook after that.

Our first step is to determine which hook best suits our needs. In order to add additional functionality to the existing `issues#show` view, we will choose the `:view_issues_show_description_bottom` hook as it allows us to insert a partial just below the standard issue details form, as indicated in the following screenshot:

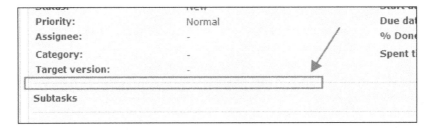

With the desired view hook identified, we need to define a listener class and tie that into our plugin initialization code.

Integrating the hook

The necessary code to define our new listener will be placed in `lib/redmine_knowledgebase/hooks.rb` and will be defined as follows:

```
module RedmineKnowledgebase
  class Hooks < Redmine::Hook::ViewListener
    render_on :view_issues_show_description_bottom,
              :partial => 'redmine_knowledgebase/hooks/view_issues_
show_description_bottom'
  end
end
```

In order to include this new class in our plugin, it just needs to be required in our `init.rb` file:

```
require_dependency 'redmine_knowledgebase/hooks'
```

Note that if we want the contents of our included classes and modules to be reloaded during development or to keep them from potentially overwriting content defined by other plugins, we should encapsulate them in a `Rails.configuration.to_prepare` block.

See `http://guides.rubyonrails.org/configuring.html#configuring-action-dispatch` for more information.

Creating the view partial

As referenced in our `hooks.rb` file, the callback for our hook is actually a view partial.

This partial will be created at `app/views/redmine_knowledgebase/hooks/_view_issues_show_description_bottom.html.erb` and can be defined as follows:

```
<% if @project.module_enabled?(:knowledgebase) %>

<div class="contextual">
<% if User.current.allowed_to?(:manage_issue_articles, @project) %>
  <%= toggle_link l(:button_add), 'new-article-form', { :focus =>
    'article_issue_to_id' } %>
<% end %>
</div>

<p><strong><%=l(:label_article_plural)%></strong></p>

<%= form_for @article, {
  :as => :article, :remote => true,
  :url => issue_articles_path(@issue),
```

```
  :method => :post,
  :html => {:id => 'new-article-form', :style => (@article ? '' :
    'display: none;')}
} do |f| %>
<%= render :partial => 'hook/issue_articles/form', :locals => {:f =>
f} %>
<% end %>


<% end %>
```

The preceding partial has been stripped down to show the bare minimum, that is, a reduced view with an **Add** button that reveals a search form on being clicked, as seen in the following screenshot:

Please note a couple of things about the preceding code:

- `@project.module_enabled?(:knowledgebase)` is used to check whether the project module provided by our plugin, as we've defined in the plugin's `init.rb` file, has been toggled in the project settings. If it is disabled, we just hide everything (the search form and any associated articles).

- `User.current.allowed_to?(:manage_issue_articles, @project)` references a project module permission we've defined in our `init.rb`.

Summary

There are a number of different types of hooks available within Redmine, but the odds are that most use-cases we'll encounter will call for view hooks.

In this chapter, we were introduced to the various types of hooks Redmine provides as well as some sample implementations of each. We also implemented a basic view hook, from which we gained a better understanding of the hook implementation and integration process.

In the next chapter, we will cover the permission registration process in detail and will discuss how plugin permissions are administered and enforced.

3

Permissions and Security

Our knowledgebase plugin adds extra content to Redmine projects in the form of categories and articles. These new content areas may contain sensitive information, which we would want to restrict certain users from accessing.

As there are different levels of users in Redmine for issue reporting and management, it is only natural that we would want to restrict access to the content in our knowledgebase plugin in a similar fashion.

This chapter will introduce the Redmine permission system and tells us how we can take advantage of it to restrict access to content areas within our plugin.

We will cover the following topics in this chapter:

- Summarizing Redmine's permissions system
- Declaring custom permissions
- Ensuring access restrictions in models, views, and controllers
- Understanding custom content access control

Summarizing Redmine's permission system

As we'll be extending Redmine's access control layer with our own custom permissions, our first course of action should be to better understand this system.

Redmine doesn't apply permissions directly to users; instead, it encapsulates permissions within roles. These roles in turn can have one to many users associated with them and are used to control access to content areas within projects, modules, and plugins.

The following screenshot shows the **Administration | Roles and permissions** view where new roles can be created, or existing roles can be modified:

Each role contains a subset of the available permissions, which are further grouped by project module, which can be toggled on or off. The following screenshot shows the **Manager** role that is available as a default in Redmine along with the available Project Permissions all toggled:

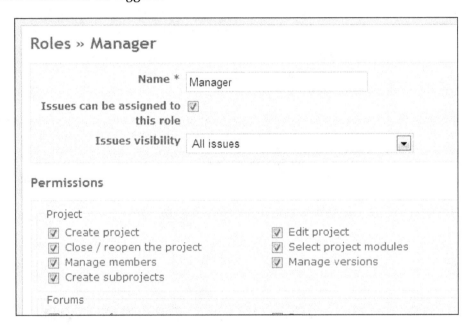

As Redmine is a project-oriented system, a project association must be made in order for the role to be applied. This is done by a project administrator or any user assigned to a role with the :manage_members permission in **Settings | Members** for the project window.

Permissions can be applied directly to users via roles, or they can be applied to groups of users. Groups are configured by a Redmine system administrator by navigating to **Administration | Groups**.

Declaring custom permissions

As we saw briefly in *Chapter 1, Introduction to Redmine Plugins*, permissions are registered in our plugin's init.rb file as part of the Redmine::Plugin.register block.

While registering a new permission, we populate a hash, which takes a controller as key, and an array of actions as the value. The syntax for this command is as follows:

```
permission(name, actions, options = {})
```

The permission helper that is available to us (plugin authors) is actually just a wrapper around Redmine::AccessControl#map, which is located in /path/to/redmine/lib/redmine/access_control.rb.

Before registering our permissions, we need to understand the two scopes of permissions that are available: global and project module.

Global permissions are a bit deceptive as they aren't actually "global" in nature. In fact, they belong to the **Project** category and are essentially just a sum of a user's permissions across all projects for which they are members.

Note that global permissions can mean different things depending on what context they're being used in:

- Permissions that are not tied to (defined within) a project module (definition)
- Permissions a user has for at least one project within the entire Redmine system (used for several cross-project features)

In order to demonstrate, let's register the following permission:

```
permission :access_global_knowledgebase, {
  :knowledgebase => :index
}
```

If we were to check the roles editor now by navigating to **Administration | Roles and Permissions** and selecting any role to edit, this new permission would in fact appear under the **Project** category.

Permissions

Project

- ☑ Create project
- ☑ Select project modules
- ☑ Create subprojects
- ☑ Edit project
- ☑ Manage members
- ☐ Access global knowledgebase

Note that for a user to be able to take advantage of this permission, they would still need to be a member of a project. If a user should *only* have access to this feature, but not additional projects, a new project should be created that all users can be a member of.

Project module permissions are declared almost identically, but are contained within a `project_module` block.

```
project_module :knowledgebase do
permission :view_kb_articles, {
  :articles     => [:index, :show, :tagged],
  :categories   => [:index, :show]
}
end
```

This block allows the permissions to be encapsulated and is therefore dependent on the project module being enabled in a project's module list before the permissions are applicable.

The previous example allows any user with the `:view_kb_articles` permission applied to be able to access the `articles#index`, `articles#show`, `articles#tagged`, `categories#index`, and `categories#show` routes.

As permissions target a controller action, we cannot provide more granular access control—for example, restricting access to individual articles—using the built-in permissions system.

Editing any role will now contain a new group for the project module
:knowledgebase with the single permission we've defined.

Ensuring access restrictions in models, views, and controllers

Now that we know how to declare and apply permissions for our plugin, we need to
ensure that those permissions are honored in the context we intended.

Checking if the current user has the permission to perform a specific action is done
using the allowed_to? function of the User model, the syntax for which is as
follows:

```
allowed_to?(action, context, options={}, &block)
```

The `action` parameter of this method can either take a parameter `Hash` (such as `:controller => "project", :action => "edit"`) or a permission `Symbol` (for example `:edit_project`).

There is also a `User` model method, `allowed_to_globally?`, that uses the same syntax, which is used to check for global permissions.

Note that, as model methods, neither `allowed_to?` nor `allowed_to_globally?` are used to actually restrict access to content areas based on defined permissions but are used to test a user instance to see if they *have* the permission to a content area. For example, in our plugin, we have a permission defined that allows users to add comments to existing knowledgebase articles.

If we check the `init.rb` file, we find the permission declaration as follows:

```
permission :comment_and_rate_articles, {
  :articles      => [:index, :show, :tagged, :rate,
                     :comment, :add_comment],
  :categories    => [:index, :show]
}
```

Comments are added via a modal dialog, which is shown when the user clicks on the **New Comment** link, which we only want to make available to authenticated users who have the permission we mentioned enabled.

In our view, we would add a check for this permission against the current user and current project, as follows:

```
<% if User.current.allowed_to?(:comment_and_rate_articles,
  @project) %>
  <%= link_to l(:label_new_comment), { :controller => "articles",
      :action => "comment", :article_id => @article, :project_id
      => @project },}, :remote => true, :method => :get %>
<% end %>
```

To actually restrict access based on the permissions we've defined for our plugin, we need to employ the `authorize` or `authorize_global` methods provided by Redmine in `ApplicationController`.

The most common implementation is to add a `before_filter` action callback to our controller that calls the `authorize` method. This method assumes that an instance variable named `@project` exists and is valid; therefore, before calling `authorize` we should call either the `find_project` or `find_project_by_project_id` method (both provided by `ApplicationController` and to be used depending on how we've set up our plugin's routing in `routes.rb`).

```
class ArticlesController < ApplicationController
  # ...

  before_filter :find_project_by_project_id, :authorize

  # ...
end
```

One of the most common uses for this type of permission check is to toggle the visibility of links. In these cases, Redmine offers a more succinct helper function, which we can use to simplify the example provided earlier by using the `link_to_if_authorized` method, as follows:

```
<%= link_to_if_authorized l(:label_new_comment), { :controller =>
"articles", :action => "comment", :article_id => @article, :project_id
=> @project }, :remote => true, :method => :get %>
```

The `link_to_if_authorized` view helper method is part of Redmine's `ApplicationHelper` module and is simply a convenience function that calls the standard Rails `link_to` method (for more information, visit http://api.rubyonrails.org/classes/ActionView/Helpers/UrlHelper.html#method-i-link_to) if the current user is authorized to access the link target's controller action.

The `authorize_for` view helper method is itself just a wrapper around the `User#allowed_to?` method. The syntax is provided as follows for reference:

```
def authorize_for(controller, action)
  User.current.allowed_to?({:controller => controller,
                            :action => action}, @project)
End
```

Unlike the `allowed_to?` and `allowed_to_globally?` model methods, or the `authorize` and `authorize_global` controller methods, the `link_to_if_authorized` and `authorize_for` helper methods should be used within the context of a view or partial.

Understanding custom content access control

The Redmine access control layer is modeled around controlling access to RESTful routes. Although this approach allows us to manage access to content areas, it falls short when it comes to actually locking down access to content itself.

The case study we're going to explore adds an additional layer of security to our knowledgebase plugin by restricting access to specific categories as well as the articles contained within those categories.

The first step we need to take is to decide how we're going to add our new permission. Ruby on Rails applications are very easy to extend using Rubygems (visit http://rubygems.org), and there are a number of access control gems available on GitHub that allow for some extremely complex permissions and access management schemes.

Instead of adding a new dependency to Redmine via an external library, since our needs are relatively simple, we're just going to extend our category model with a user whitelist.

The goals of this whitelist are to:

* Allow administrative users with the proper permissions the ability to manage whitelist membership
* Ensure content is not visible to members who are not explicitly added to a whitelist
* Ignore whitelists if no members have been added

The plugin that we're extending is hosted at https://github.com/alexbevi/ redmine_knowledgebase, and any references to the models, views, or controllers are assumed to be derived from the code of the 3.0 developer and 3.0 final Versions.

As we're extending an existing model, we'll add a migration in the standard Ruby on Rails fashion and put the new file in our plugin's db/migrate directory. All our migration will do is add a new column to the category model.

```
class AddUserWhitelistToCategories < ActiveRecord::Migration
  def change
    add_column :kb_categories, :user_whitelist, :string,
      :default => ""
  end
end
```

For a refresher on Ruby on Rails migrations, visit http://guides.rubyonrails.org/migrations.html.

In order to actually apply the change, we need to rerun the Redmine plugin migration Rake task from the root of the Redmine deployment directory.

```
$ rake redmine:plugins:migrate
Migrating redmine_knowledgebase (Knowledgebase)...
==  AddUserWhitelistToCategories: migrating ===============================
======
-- add_column(:kb_categories, :user_whitelist, :string, {:default=>""})
   -> 0.0011s
==  AddUserWhitelistToCategories: migrated (0.0013s)
==========================
```

Managing user whitelists

The new field we added to our category model will take a comma-separated string of user IDs that represents users we are explicitly granting access to.

Before we can start adding any users, we need to ensure that access to this functionality is properly restricted. We'll begin by adding a new permission to our plugin's init.rb file.

```
permission :manage_category_whitelist, {
  :articles      => :index,
  :categories    => [:index, :show, :edit, :update]
}
```

Using this new permission, the form partial that is used to create and edit new categories will be extended to check whether the current user has the appropriate permission to manage user whitelists.

```
<% if User.current.allowed_to?(:manage_category_whitelist
  , @project) %>
  <%= render :partial => "categories/members" %>
<% end %>
```

The contents of the_members.html.erb partial referenced in the preceding code is included here as well, in order to provide a more complete picture of the implementation:

```
<%  whitelisted = @category.user_whitelist.split(",") %>
<p>
```

```
    <label><%= l(:label_user_whitelist) %></label>
<% @project.users.sort.each do |user| %>
    <%= check_box_tag 'user_whitelist[]', user.id, whitelisted.
include?(user.id.to_s) %> <%= h user %><br/>
<% end %>
</p>
```

As the following screenshot illustrates, the users who have been explicitly granted access to the project our knowledgebase plugin is enabled on are presented in a checkbox list under a **User whitelist** section:

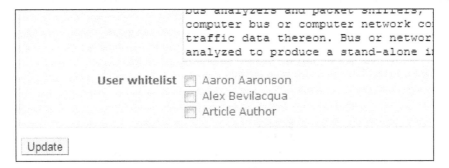

Our category creation and update view now contains a section for whitelist management based on the associated project's user list, as can be seen in the previous screenshot.

In order to actually save the changes when **Update** is clicked, the update method of the CategoriesController needs to be adjusted slightly.

After the category is loaded, but before the attributes are updated, we'll just inject a quick assignment of the submitted data.

```
@category.user_whitelist = if params["user_whitelist"].blank?
  ""
else
  params["user_whitelist"].join(",")
end
```

Restricting access via whitelists

Now that administrators have the ability to add and update category whitelists, we need to update our views in order to disable access to specific content.

The choice to implement a whitelist (as opposed to a blacklist) is to ensure that the default behavior would reflect the standard permissive nature the plugin had before we implemented this change.

Since the default access logic is to allow all unless a whitelist is explicitly defined, we're going to add a `blacklisted?` method to our category model to help us determine whether a user should be allowed to view the category and its contents.

```
def blacklisted?(user)
  return false if self.user_whitelist.blank?

  whitelisted = self.user_whitelist.split(",").include?
    (user.id.to_s)
  !whitelisted
end
```

Since our categories are configured as nested sets, we'll need to check our whitelists when fetching the root nodes as well as the subsequent children.

In both cases, the code would be modified in a similar fashion.

```
@categories = @project.categories.where(:parent_id
  => nil).delete_if { |cat| cat.blacklisted?(User.current) }
```

The `delete_if` method is added to the standard category lookup above in order to prune out any content the user doesn't have access to.

Enforcing the whitelist

The content we removed in the previous section only limits non-whitelisted users from *seeing* the restricted content.

If they were to navigate directly to the URL of a page they weren't supposed to see, that content would still be displayed as there is no logic to prevent them from accessing it.

To prevent unauthorized access to a category, we need to modify the `show` method of the `CategoriesController` in order to check whether a user is blacklisted before the page is rendered.

```
if @category.blacklisted?(User.current)
  render_403
  return false
end
```

 This can also be enforced by moving the necessary functionality to a separate method and then calling that from `before_filter`.

If a user tries to access a category they have been denied access to, they will now be presented with a standard access denied message.

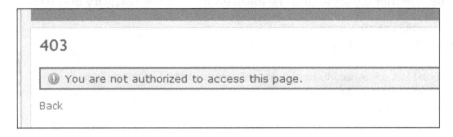

The same logic should be applied to the articles contained within categories. If a user tries to access an article directly but the category the article belongs to has a whitelist, the user should be redirected away from the restricted content.

This is accomplished almost identically to how `CategoriesController` was modified, but in this case, we'll update the `show` method of `ArticlesController`.

```
if @article.category.blacklisted?(User.current)
  render_403
  return false
end
```

The example that is provided here is meant to illustrate how a basic content-specific access control layer can be implemented using as much of Redmine's internals as possible.

If this method is going to be used in production systems where sensitive information needs to be protected in a more granular fashion, a couple of deficiencies need to be listed as they were glossed over:

- This example does not validate siblings or parents in the hierarchy when rendering the category tree
- This example doesn't limit Redmine search results based on whitelist membership

Summary

Restricting access to various content areas and limiting what users can do with existing content are the primary functions of Redmine's permission system.

In this chapter, we learned how Redmine manages permissions, how we can add our own controllers and actions to a permissions list, and how to enforce these permissions in our views.

We also explored a case study and provided a whitelist approach to restricting content in a more granular fashion than Redmine provides in its core libraries.

In the next chapter, we'll be adding file attachments to our plugin's models.

4
Attaching Files to Models

One very common extension we end up having to implement in our models, be it in Redmine or in another project, is the ability to attach files. As we're working on a knowledgebase plugin, our articles could be made more informative by allowing external files to be attached as reference items.

If we were writing our own Ruby on Rails application, the process of adding file attachment capabilities is generally delegated to an external library or gem such as paperclip (`https://github.com/thoughtbot/paperclip`) or carrierwave (`https://github.com/carrierwaveuploader/carrierwave`).

Redmine has conveniently abstracted this all away for us, which makes adding file upload and attachment features almost no work at all.

We will cover the following topics in this chapter:

- How our models are updated with the internal `acts_as_attachable` plugin
- How to implement the existing file attachment view partial and what options it takes
- Using the `link_to_attachments` view helper
- How to manage attachment permissions and how to further restrict the deletion of attachments

Model preparation

Redmine has implemented a number of internal plugins, which are located under `/path/to/redmine/lib/plugins`.

These plugins follow the traditional Rails naming idiom of `acts_as_*` (for more information on this topic, visit `http://guides.rubyonrails.org/plugins.html#add-an-acts-as-method-to-active-record`), which implies that we'll be including a class level method, which is named the same as the plugin.

The class we'll be extending is the model that our knowledgebase plugin uses to manage articles.

```
class KbArticle < ActiveRecord::Base
  validates :title, :presence => true
  validates :category_id, :presence => true

  belongs_to :project
  belongs_to :category, :class_name => "KbCategory"
  belongs_to :author,   :class_name => 'User',
                        :foreign_key => 'author_id'

  # class method from Redmine::Acts::Attachable::ClassMethods
  acts_as_attachable

  # class definition continues ...
End
```

By including `acts_as_attachable` in our class, a has-many association is established and a number of instance methods are automatically injected into the class. These methods are used by the view helpers in order to validate and save attachments.

A couple of handy helper functions provided by `acts_as_attachable` are:

- `attachments_visible?(user=User.current)`
- `attachments_deletable?(user=User.current)`

Both methods check whether a Redmine user has the permission to perform a certain action on an attachment that has been added to an associated model.

These permissions are covered in detail in the *Managing attachment permissions* section later in this chapter.

The default permissions are formed by joining a prefix with a pluralized and underscored representation of the model's name that `acts_as_attachable` is being added to. For example, our article model would have `:view_kb_article` and `:edit_kb_article` by default.

Note that our model must respond to `self.project` either by having a project association (`belongs_to`) or by means of an instance method. This is due to the `attachments_visible?` and `attachments_deleteable?` methods using the `User#allowed_to?` method to validate access and interaction with a model's attachments.

Enabling attachments in our views

Adding multiple file attachment capabilities to our article creation and update form is also simple and straightforward. To make our implementation even easier, Redmine already has a styled and structured sample available in the issue management code that we can reuse.

The following code snippet needs to be copied and pasted into the form (or form partial) that we're using to create and edit articles. Assuming we're using the standard Rails method of building forms using `FormBuilder` (visit `http://api.rubyonrails.org/classes/ActionView/Helpers/FormBuilder.html`), the following code would need to be inserted within a view's `form_for` block:

```
<div class="box">
  <p>
    <label><%=l(:label_attachment_plural)%></label>
    <%= render :partial => 'attachments/form' %>
  </p>
</div>
```

This incorporates the stock Redmine view partial that allows files to be uploaded asynchronously and attached to our model.

The preceding partial adds an additional form field array called `attachments`, which takes attachments via `file_field_tag`. Multiple files can be attached at once as the partial we're using dynamically adds each file to the form (see `/path/to/redmine/app/views/attachments/_form.html.erb` for the full implementation).

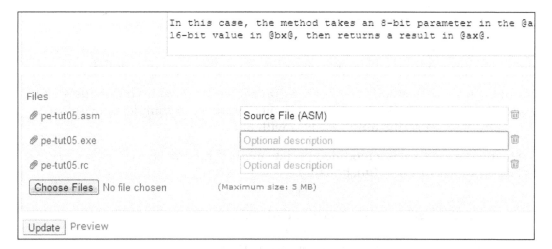

The attached files can also be deleted and have optional descriptions provided.

 Note that the **Maximum size** value is based on the value provided at **Administration | Settings** under the **General** tab in the **Maximum attachment size** field.

Controller modifications to accommodate attachments

Since we're using the standard Redmine view partials to manage our attachments, when a new article is created or updated, attachments are submitted to our controller in an attachments collection, which is available from `params[:attachments]`:

```
"attachments"=>
{"1"=>
  {"filename"=>"8748OS_04_01.png",
    "description"=>"",
    "token"=>"4.f5bd5eabd62c9ec71b427d8195f18285"},
  "2"=>
    {"filename"=>"8748OS_04_02.png",
      "description"=>"",
      "token"=>"5.f8bd02cfcb83aba081bf69ac06fdb085"},
  "3"=>
    {"filename"=>"8748OS_04_03.png",
      "description"=>"",
      "token"=>"6.80b7dd688925171341b4004fc9ddcf69"}}
```

The actual file uploads are handled asynchronously by Redmine before we even submit the form, but we still have to associate these files with our model.

One of the instance methods that `acts_as_attachable` provides our models with is `save_attachments`. This can be used in our controller to complete the upload process by associating the uploaded files with our model.

The following example is a modified update method for our `ArticlesController` that incorporates this new functionality:

```
def update
  @article = KbArticle.find(params[:id])
  # ...
  if @article.update_attributes(params[:article])
    @article.save_attachments(params[:attachments])
    render_attachment_warning_if_needed(@article)
```

```
    # ...
    redirect_to { :action => 'show', :id => @article.id,
        :project_id => @project }
  end
end
```

We have included a call to `render_attachment_warning_if_needed(obj)` in the previous example as a convenience. This method is not part of `acts_as_attachable` but can be added to any plugin's controller as it is a method of Redmine's `ApplicationController`. It adds a warning to the Rails Flash (visit `http://api.rubyonrails.org/classes/ActionDispatch/Flash.html`) if any attachments remain unsaved.

Listing and managing attachments

Redmine provides a view partial for listing the existing attachments on a model as well. In order to quickly implement this functionality, the `/path/to/redmine/app/views/attachments/_links.html.erb` partial can be plugged into any view and passed a collection of attachments as follows:

```
<%= render :partial => 'attachments/links',
  :locals  => { :attachments => @article.attachments,
  :options => { :deletable => User.current.logged? }
          } %>
```

This will change the view as shown in the following screenshot:

In addition to the attachments collection that is required, the `links` partial also accepts an `options` hash. This hash only accepts the following keys:

- `:author`: If the value evaluates to true, the attachment author is listed along with the timestamp of when the attachment was created

- :deletable: If the value evaluates to true, a delete link will be rendered, which allows the current user the ability to permanently remove the attachment

- :thumbnails: When this option is provided and evaluates to true, attachment thumbnails will be displayed if enabled by the system administrator (**Administration | Settings | Display | Display attachment thumbnails**)

The :deleteable option is an all-or-nothing option for the entire attachment collection that is passed to the partial view. As such, if we're looking to implement a more granular security setup, we could render the attachments/links partial more than once with filtered collections.

```
<% @article.attachments.group_by { |f| File.extname(f.filename).
include?("exe") }.each do |group| %>
  <%= render :partial => 'attachments/links',
    :locals  => { :attachments => group[1],
    :options => { :deletable => User.current.logged? && group[0] }
} %>
<% end %>
```

This example will group the attachments collection based on whether or not the filename includes the .exe extension, and if it does, will allow deletion.

As the grouping approach leaves a visible separation between groups, another option would be to clone the partial provided in the Redmine source and extend it according to our specific criteria.

For a quicker implementation of the attachments/links partial, Redmine provides a method in AttachmentsHelper:

```
link_to_attachments(container, options = {})
```

This view helper method checks the container (model instance) for any attachments, and renders the attachments/links partial if any exist.

The helper method here takes a container that has attachments associated with it. In this case, we would pass our `@article` instance, not the attachments collections directly.

The implementation we just described using the `attachment/links` partial directly could now be shortened to something along the lines of this:

```
<%= link_to_attachments @article,
  :thumbnails => true,
  :author     => true %>
```

This example omits the `:deletable` option but provides a couple of additional options.

When `:thumbnails` is provided, if an attachment is an image (see the `image?` method in `/path/to/redmine/app/models/attachment.rb`), a thumbnail representation of the attachment will be included below the standard attachment links.

The `:author` option is used to toggle whether the name of the user who originally uploaded the attachment should be listed along with the attachment.

Managing attachment permissions

Adding attachment functionality to our models through `acts_ast_attachable` comes with two preconfigured management permissions: a view permission and a delete permission.

In order to properly implement these permissions, they would have to be declared along with our plugin's other named permissions in our `init.rb` file. You can refer to *Chapter 1, Introduction to Redmine Plugins*, for a quick refresher on declaring custom permissions.

Both of these permissions are dynamically generated based on the class name of the model we've added attachments to.

The format of both the view and delete permissions by default are:

```
"view_#{self.name.pluralize.underscore}".to_sym
"delete_#{self.name.pluralize.underscore}".to_sym
```

As our knowledgebase articles are declared in a KbArticle class, the resulting generated permissions would be :view_kb_articles and :delete_kb_articles.

If we have attachments in an article and try to delete them without properly declaring and assigning these permissions, Redmine's authorization system will reject the request and display the following output:

```
Started DELETE "/attachments/10" for 127.0.0.1 at 2013-12-17 21:50:12
-0500
Processing by AttachmentsController#destroy as HTML
  ...
Filter chain halted as :delete_authorize rendered or redirected
Completed 403 Forbidden in 32ms (Views: 19.6ms | ActiveRecord: 2.2ms)
```

If we prefer to supply our own permissions to acts_as_attachable, this is done in our model by providing our own permission symbols to either :delete_permission or :view_permission.

```
class KbArticle < ActiveRecord::Base
  # ...
  acts_as_attachable :delete_permission => :manage_articles
  # ...
end
```

In this example, instead of declaring a :delete_kb_articles permission in our init.rb file, we would instead declare a :manage_articles permission. This permission would subsequently be used by attachments_deleteable?(user) when checking to see whether the current user is allowed to delete an attachment.

Summary

In this chapter, we covered the basics of quickly adding the ability to attach files to our models and how our views and partials could be extended with Redmine's existing file attachment partials.

We also learned about the various options that are available to `acts_as_attachable` as well as how attachment permissions are managed.

In the next chapter, we'll be making our models searchable.

5
Making Models Searchable

Our knowledgebase plugin is meant to facilitate the creation and management of large quantities of categorized information. Once this system grows to a certain size, it will no longer be feasible to simply navigate directly to content when a user is trying to find something generic.

Redmine provides an extremely versatile search system for all of its own internal models, which can easily be extended to plugin models through the application of a couple of built-in plugins.

This chapter will introduce the Redmine search subsystem and how our models can quickly hook into it.

We will cover the following topics in this chapter:

- Initializing our plugin to be included in Redmine searches
- Setting up the required result formatting through `acts_as_event`
- Getting our model ready to actually be searched using `acts_as_searchable`
- How Redmine permissions limit the availability of search functionality
- How custom permissions can be used to override search results

Registering our plugin

The first step to setting up our plugin to be incorporated into Redmine's internal search is to register our model.

This is done in our plugin's `init.rb` file anywhere outside the `Redmine::Plugin.register` block, using the following code:

```
Redmine::Search.available_search_types << 'kb_articles'
```

Redmine is now aware of our plugin's model and will be looking for it whenever a project or global search is requested.

Preparing our models to be searched

The `acts_as_event` plugin is used internally by Redmine in order to maintain consistency between various models that need to be grouped together.

In our case, the models that are being searched need to have `acts_as_event` implemented in order to determine what constitutes a title, how the title will be formatted, what the description field is, and so on.

Note that `acts_as_event` is a dependency of `acts_as_searchable`; therefore, if it isn't included in our model, Redmine will crash when a search is attempted.

The function prototype for `acts_as_event` is a standard class method that accepts an options hash:

```
def acts_as_event(options = {})
```

As we'll be marking our knowledgebase articles as searchable, we will begin by adding `acts_as_event` to our article model:

```
class KbArticle < ActiveRecord::Base
  # ...

  acts_as_event :datetime    => :updated_at,
                :description => :summary,
                :title => Proc.new { |o| "#{l(:label_title_articles)}
##{o.id} - #{o.title}" },
                :url     => Proc.new { |o| { :controller => 'articles',
                                             :action => 'show',
                                             :id => o.id,
                                             :project_id => o.project }
                }


  # ...
end
```

The `acts_as_event` options hash can be initialized with the following keys:

- `:datetime`: The field within our model that will be used as a timestamp. The default is `:created_on`. Its value can be either `Proc` or `Symbol`.

- `:title`: The model field that will be used when rendering an event title. The default value is `:title`. Its value can be either `Proc` or `Symbol`.

- `:description`: The model fields that will be used when displaying additional information about an entry. The default value is `:description`. Its value can be either `Proc` or `Symbol`.

- `:author`: The model field that will be used when author information about an entry is displayed. The default value is `:author`. Its value can be either `Proc` or `Symbol`.

- `:url`: The URL to the record an event refers to. The default value is `{ :controller => 'welcome' }`. This value can be `Proc`, a `Symbol`, `Hash`, or `String`.

- `:type`: Used by other plugins to filter certain types of events (for example, see the `acts_as_activity_provider` class method to find events in the Redmine source). The default value is the result of `self.name.underscore.dasherize` (for example, `kb-article`).

- `:group`: Used by the `ActivitiesHelper` when sorting activity events. The default group value is `self` (the model `acts_as_event` is implemented), but can be overridden by providing a value to this option. See `/path/to/redmine/app/helpers/activities_helper.rb` for more information.

In order to implement `acts_as_searchable`, the bare minimum options required in order to ensure that searching will function are `:datetime`, `:description`, `:title`, and `:url`.

Configuring search options

Once `acts_as_event` has been implemented, we can finish preparing our model by implementing `acts_as_searchable`.

As with all previous internal plugins, the class extension needs to be included in the model we will be making searchable.

```
class KbArticle < ActiveRecord::Base
  validates :title, :presence => true
  validates :category_id, :presence => true
  # ..
  acts_as_searchable :columns => [ "#{table_name}.title", "#{table_
name}.content"],
```

```
                        :include => [ :project ],
                        :order_column => "#{table_name}.id",
                        :date_column => "#{table_name}.created_at"
    # ..
end
```

This example allows our article model to be incorporated into Redmine's default search infrastructure, with article titles and the article contents being used as searchable targets.

The `acts_as_searchable` plugin takes a number of optional values in the form of a hash. The most common values are as follows:

- `:columns`: This specifies the column or array of columns to search.

- `:project_key`: This is the project foreign key. The default value assumes that the model we're attaching `acts_as_attachable` to has a `project_id` field defined in the schema.

- `:date_column`: This is name of the datetime column. The default value is `created_on`.

- `:sort_order`: This is used to sort a column using it's column name. The default value is either the previously defined `:date_column` or implied `created_on` column.

- `:permission`: This is the permission required to search the model. This optional property is used to define a custom permission value that a user must have in order to be able to search our model. The default value is in the format `:view_"model"`, so in our case, it would be `:view_kb_articles`. If a permission is defined and the current user doesn't have that permission applied explicitly, the model we're making searchable won't show up as a filter option in the Redmine search.

If the user didn't have the appropriate permissions, there would not be an option for **Knowledgebase articles**.

Filtering search results using custom permissions

In *Chapter 3, Permissions and Security,* we introduced a custom permission model that allowed us to whitelist users against certain knowledgebase categories.

As this is functionality that we added to the system, Redmine doesn't understand how this content needs to be filtered.

To illustrate the process, first we'll ensure that one of our categories has an explicit whitelist defined.

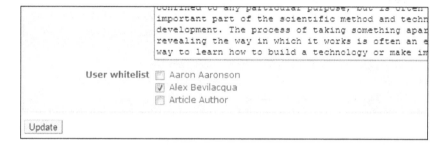

This category currently contains a number of articles that contain references to viruses, which is what we'll be using as a search term.

If we were to execute this search as the current user, the results would contain all articles that contain a reference to the word "virus" either in the title, or in the content of the article. This is shown in the following screenshot:

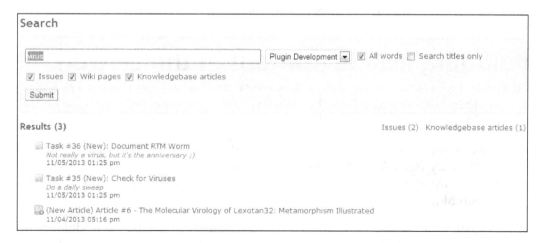

If the user wasn't on the whitelist, trying to select the article would result in an error, which is the desired behavior in this situation. This situation violates our security policy though, as it exposes some information about the article even without allowing the user to access it. A much better solution would be for the results of the search to not even include content we've explicitly revoked access to.

Since the `acts_as_searchable` extension adds a search method, we'll override this method in order to ensure our custom permissions are applied to the results.

```
# override the acts_as_searchable search method in order to filter
  the results
# by category permissions
def self.search(tokens, projects=nil, options={})
  # the results are presented as an array with two entries:
  # [0] => an array of the models returned in the search result
  # [1] => the count of the results
  result = super(tokens, projects, options)
  # first we want to check if any of the results shouldn't be
  # visible to the current user
  result[0].delete_if { |article| article.category.blacklisted?(User.
current) }
  # update the total count just in case the results were further
    filtered
  result[1] = result[0].length

  result
end
```

Although this accomplishes the desired result of reducing the result set to only content our users should see, it does so *after* the search has already been executed.

Including article content in the search

In the search we previously executed, there were two issue items returned as well as one knowledgebase article. When the search results were rendered, the issue items contained description text with highlighted matches, but our article didn't.

When we first set up `acts_as_event`, the `:description` field was mapped to the article's summary field. As this field is optional in our plugin and may not always be populated, we want to change this to something that will be present in all articles we'll be searching.

In order to do this, the implementation of `acts_as_event` needs to be updated with a new description mapping of `:description` to `:content`.

```
class KbArticle < ActiveRecord::Base
  # ...
  acts_as_event
    :datetime    => :updated_at,
    :description => :content,
    :title => Proc.new { |o| "#{l(:label_title_articles)} ##{o.id}
      - #{o.title}" },
    :url    => Proc.new { |o| { :controller => 'articles',
                                :action => 'show',
                                :id => o.id,
                                :project_id => o.project } }
  # ...
end
```

Once this has been done, if we run the search for "virus" again, the results will contain the article contents as well, as shown in the following screenshot:

Results (3)   Issues (2) Knowledgebase articles (1)

  Task #36 (New): Document RTM Worm
  Not really a virus, but it's the anniversary ;)
  11/05/2013 01:25 pm

  Task #35 (New): Check for Viruses
  Do a daily sweep
  11/05/2013 01:25 pm

  Article #6 - The Molecular Virology of Lexotan32: Metamorphism Illustrated
  Introduction This paper is a direct descen ... rding the metamorphic engine of the W32.Evol virus. I advise you to take a look at it before re ... paper is the special engine of the Lexotan32 virus. The virus was released in 29A#6 Virus Magazine in 2002, the Annus Mirabilis of metamorphic viruses. The virus was created by the prolific VX coder, Vecna, ... d further elaborate on the genealogy of this virus, but I think it is sufficient to say that this virus is a culmination of many of the techniques d ... ght that this paper would be written, as the virus was released with its original source code, ... in amount of generations (as in the W32.Evol virus). Several viruses solved this problem in creative ways; The TMC virus...
  11/04/2013 05:16 pm

Summary

No matter how big or how small our knowledgebase is, having the ability to search for content makes the system much more useful to our end users.

In this chapter, we learned how the Redmine search system can be extended to include our custom models in search results as well as how to format the results to be consistent with other Redmine searchable items.

In the next chapter, we'll be adding our articles and categories to Redmine's activity stream.

6
Interacting with the Activity Stream

One of the most useful features of Redmine is the ability to provide a generic, timestamp-sorted listing of the happenings within a project (or all projects) using the activity stream.

Whether we're looking for changesets, issue updates, news, a document of forum submissions, or any other Redmine project module update, the activity stream will provide a summarized representation of any content changes.

For our plugin to fully integrate into a Redmine project as a project module, any update we create should also be reflected within the project's activity stream.

This chapter will introduce the activity stream and how it can be leveraged by plugin authors in order to provide activity summaries in line with other Redmine activities.

We will cover the following topics in this chapter:

- A summary of Redmine's activity listing subsystem
- An overview of the `acts_as_activity_provider` internal plugin
- How the `acts_as_event` plugin applies to `acts_as_activity_provider`
- How to customize activity stream entries through `acts_as_event`

Overview of the activity stream

A project's activity stream is directly accessible by navigating to the **Activity** tab. Once selected, all available activities are summarized, including present activities.

If we wish to see all activities from all available projects, either go to **Projects** in the application bar and then select **Overall Activity** or navigate directly to `http://localhost:3000/activity`.

Any model within Redmine that implements the `acts_as_activity_provider` plugin can be displayed in the following listing:

The preceding screenshot is taken from the official bug tracker for the Ruby language (`https://bugs.ruby-lang.org/activity`).

The screenshot illustrates the two main components of an activity stream:

- The activity filter list
- The activity stream

The filter list allows users to select the project modules that are available in the stream, assuming their activity providers are defined.

The stream is a list sorted in reverse chronology and comprises all the items that have been selected from the filter list and occur within the range that has been defined by the system administrator.

 For system administrators, the activity stream limit can be set in `http://localhost:3000/settings`, in the setting entry for **Days displayed on project activity** under the **General** tab.

Preparing our model

We're going to adapt our KbArticle model so that new articles will be listed in the activity stream of any project with a knowledgebase.

In *Chapter 5, Making Models Searchable*, we introduced the acts_as_event plugin as a prerequisite to use the acts_as_searchable plugin; it also serves as a prerequisite for acts_as_activity_provider.

If we implement acts_as_activity_provider without acts_as_event and try to load an activity stream, Redmine will crash with a NoMethodError exception:

```
NoMethodError (undefined method `event_datetime' for
  #<KbArticle:0x000000042b9428>)
```

The example we provided in the previous chapter is being cited here for continuity:

```
class KbArticle < ActiveRecord::Base
  # ...

  acts_as_event :datetime    => :updated_at,
                :description => :summary,
                :title => Proc.new { |o| "#{l(:label_title_articles)}
##{o.id} - #{o.title}" },
                :url    => Proc.new { |o| { :controller => 'articles',
                                            :action => 'show',
                                            :id => o.id,
                                            :project_id => o.project }
                }

  # ...
end
```

Note that if your model uses more than one internal Redmine plugin that relies on acts_as_event, you don't have to implement acts_as_event more than once.

Registering our model

Our model is now capable of integrating with the Redmine activity stream; however, Redmine is still unaware of our model in this context.

In order to have our model's events actually represented in the activity stream, our plugin initialization file needs to be updated.

```
Redmine::Activity.register :kb_articles
```

The preceding entry needs to be added to our `init.rb` file after the `Redmine::Plugin.register` block.

Now that we have registered our model with Redmine, the implementation of `acts_as_activity_provider` will produce results in a project's activity stream.

Configuring an activity provider

For a model to be designated as an activity provider, we'll need to implement the `acts_as_activity_provider` plugin that comes with Redmine.

The method's signature for this plugin is as follows:

```
def acts_as_activity_provider(options = {})
```

If we're looking to dive directly into the source code for the plugin, it is available as part of our Redmine installation at `/path/to/redmine/lib/plugins/acts_as_activity_provider/lib/acts_as_activity_provider.rb`.

The `acts_as_activity_provider` plugin is another class extension plugin and requires us to call the `acts_as_activity_provider` method within our model's class definition along with some parameters as follows:

```
class KbArticle < ActiveRecord::Base
  # ...

  acts_as_activity_provider :find_options => {:include => :project},
                            :author_key   => :author_id,
                            :type         => 'kb_articles',
                            :timestamp    => :updated_at

  # ...
end
```

The `acts_as_activity_provider` method takes a hash as a parameter. This options hash accepts a number of potential keys, although none of them is strictly required due to the default values being available for most. Let's have a look at them:

- `:type`: Using this, multiple event types can be represented in an activity stream, and therefore, unique identifiers are required to keep these events separated. The default value of this option is the model's class name, which is underscored and pluralized. For example, our model name is `KbArticle`, so the default name will be `kb_articles`.

- `:permission`: This is used if a custom permission has been defined for a user to view our model's content in an activity stream. If a permission value has been defined as nil, the default value of `:view_project` will be used instead. Even though a default value is available, it is a good practice to provide a permission named by us as it better isolates our plugin from core Redmine. For more in-depth coverage of permissions, see *Chapter 3, Permissions and Security*.

- `:timestamp`: This is the `datetime` field that is used to establish a sort order for the model. If no value is provided, a default value of the model's `created_on` field is used.

- `:author_key`: This is a symbol that identifies the field within our model that contains an ID for the user that created a new record. This value needs to map to a valid Redmine user.

- `:find_options`: This is used if additional filtration details need to be provided in order to limit the activity stream results. The values provided to the `:find_options` hash should be standard `ActiveRecord` query options. For example, `find_options` in our previous sample implementation contains `:find_options => { :include => :project }`, which allows us to name the project association that will be loaded alongside our model.

Now that we have our activity provider defined and implemented, the **Activity** tab of any project in which we've enabled the knowledgebase functionality will contain knowledgebase articles in the stream.

Customizing activity entries

The `acts_as_event` plugin mentioned previously is being used to provide a consistent representation of our data across multiple models by defining common elements.

The ability to provide `Proc` as a parameter in most fields (see *Chapter 5, Making Models Searchable*) means that we can include executable code within our declaration.

In the sample provided earlier in this chapter, we listed article titles as a combination of their ID value as well as their title:

```
acts_as_event :title => Proc.new { |o| "#{l(:label_title_articles)}
  ##{o.id} - #{o.title}" }
```

Activity

From 10/12/2013 to 11/10/2013

11/05/2013

 01:25 pm **Plugin Development - Task #36 (New): Document RTM Worm**
Not really a virus, but it's the anniversary ;)
Alex Bevilacqua

 01:25 pm **Plugin Development - Task #35 (New): Check for Viruses**
Do a daily sweep
Alex Bevilacqua

11/04/2013

 05:17 pm **Plugin Development - Article #7 - Defeating HyperUnpackMe2 With an** Processor Module
1.0 Introduction
This article is about breaking modern executable protectors. The target, a crackme know
Hype...
Alex Bevilacqua

 05:16 pm **Plugin Development - Article #6 - The Molecular Virology of Lexotan32:**

We're already using a procedure in order to build the link title, so we can take this even further and append additional information.

In the following example, we'll attach the article tag list to the article title:

```
acts_as_event :title => Proc.new { |o| tags = (o.tag_list.blank?)
? nil : "[#{o.tag_list.join(', ')}]"; "
#{l(:label_title_articles)} ##{o.id} - #{o.title} #{tags}" }
```

Activity
From 10/12/2013 to 11/10/2013

11/11/2013

 10:56 pm **Article #8 - Execute Another Program [code, asm, tasm, source]**
Compile with tasm....
Alex Bevilacqua

The link to the article in the activity stream now contains the individual tags following the article title.

Note that if we change how an element in `acts_as_event` is being formatted, this change will also be reflected in all search results.

 Unlike `acts_as_activity_provider`, the `acts_as_event` plugin can only be included once per model.

Summary

The activity stream is an extremely useful feature of Redmine and is generally the starting point for a lot of users when they enter the system.

Having our plugins register with the activity stream provides greater value to end users as they can quickly see what has been happening within our plugin from the same screen they would be following up with other plugins and core system events.

In this chapter, we learned how to include our plugin in a project's activity stream as well as how to tweak the formatting of the results.

In the next chapter, we'll explore plugin configuration management.

7

Managing Plugin Settings

As we continue to add features and functionalities to our plugin, the need for custom configuration also becomes more apparent. It is likely that system administrators will not need all the bells and whistles at all times, or they may need to fine-tune one thing or another. Having such flexibility results in our plugin becoming even more appealing.

Redmine provides plugin authors with tools that facilitate the process of managing plugin-specific settings, which we'll explore in this chapter.

We will cover the following topics in this chapter:

- How to initialize our plugin with settings and default values
- The configuration of the settings partial
- The use of custom settings in controllers and views

An overview of Redmine's global plugin settings

Redmine provides plugin authors with an integrated configuration system in order to simplify the management of configuration values:

Redmine CRM plugin This is a CRM plugin for Redmine that can be used to track contacts and deals information http://redminecrm.com	RedmineCRM	3.1.2-light	Configure
Redmine Invoices plugin Plugin for track invoices http://redminecrm.com/projects/invoices	RedmineCRM	2.1.0-light	Configure
Dropbox Attachment Storage Use Dropbox for attachment storage https://github.com/alexbevi/redmine_dropbox_attachments	Alex Bevilacqua	2.0.1	Configure
Gist Embed Defines macro to embed Github Gists into Redmine	Alex Dergachev	0.1.0	
Knowledgebase A plugin for Redmine that adds knowledgebase functionality https://github.com/alexbevi/redmine_knowledgebase	Alex Bevilacqua	3.0.0-devel1	Configure

Plugin settings are only available to Redmine users with administrator privileges. For these users, a summary of all plugins is available at `http://localhost:3000/admin/plugins`.

If a plugin has been configured to provide an administrator with a settings view, a **Configure** link will be available.

The information that is displayed for each plugin in the list is pulled from the `name`, `author`, `author_url`, `description`, `url`, and `version` attributes that were provided to the `Redmine::Plugin.register` block in each plugin's `init.rb` file.

 As of Redmine 2.3.4, which was released on November 17, 2013, the plugin settings management interface is only available for global configuration. There are no functionalities provided in order to manage custom per-project settings.

Enabling settings management

In *Chapter 1*, *Introduction to Redmine Plugins*, we were introduced to the Redmine plugin's initialization file as well as some of the attributes, methods, and helpers available to plugin authors.

The `settings` attribute was presented as a way for plugin settings to be initialized as well as a configuration partial view to be defined:

```
Redmine::Plugin.register :redmine_knowledgebase do
  # ...

  settings :default => {
    :sort_category_tree      => 1,
    :show_category_totals    => 1,
    :summary_limit           => 5,
    :disable_article_summaries => 0
  }, :partial => 'redmine_knowledgebase/knowledgebase_settings'

  # ...
end
```

Our plugin's `settings` field is initialized with a hash that expects two keys:

- `:default`: This key expects a hash, which will be used to initialize our plugin's settings values to defaults that will be presented on first use. Once a configuration value has been explicitly set, the default values are no longer used.

- :partial: This holds a relative path to a partial view within our plugin that can be used to set configuration and settings values. Using the previous example of `redmine_knowledgebase/knowledgebase_settings`, the location of the actual partial view will be `/path/to/redmine/plugins/ redmine_knowledgebase/app/views/redmine_knowledgebase/_ knowledgebase_settings.html.erb`.

> A generic value (for example, settings, config) should not be used as it can potentially be overwritten by another plugin using the same name. A good approach is to place your settings partial view in a subfolder named after your plugin; in our case, `redmine_knowledgebase/ knowledgebase_settings`.

Configuration management

The partial view we defined when initializing our plugin's `settings` field will be rendered when an administrator clicks on the **Configure** link for our plugin:

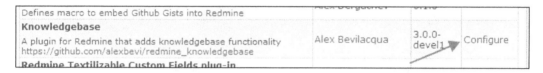

The partial that we'll create will be made up of a number of groups. Each group represents a settings key that we want to update a value for.

The fields that we'll define will be a subset of a predefined form, which is rendered if our plugin has defined a partial to be used for configuration. This partial is injected into the form at `/path/to/redmine/app/views/settings/plugin.html.erb`.

As the form tag has already been defined, all we have to provide are input tags that capture our settings, values. For this to work properly, we name the input fields `settings[our_setting_name]`.

```erb
<p>
  <%= label_tag :settings_sort_category_tree, l(:allow_sort_category_
tree) %>
  <%= check_box_tag 'settings[sort_category_tree]', 1, @
settings[:sort_category_tree] %>
</p>
<p>
  <%= label_tag :settings_show_category_totals, l(:show_category_
totals) %>
```

```
  <%= check_box_tag 'settings[show_category_totals]', 1, @
settings[:show_category_totals] %>
</p>
<p>
  <%= label_tag :settings_summary_limit, l(:summary_item_limit) %>
  <%= text_field_tag "settings[summary_limit]", @settings[:summary_
limit] %>
</p>
<p>
  <%= label_tag :settings_disable_article_summaries, l(:disable_
article_summaries) %>
  <%= check_box_tag 'settings[disable_article_summaries]', 1, @
settings[:disable_article_summaries] %>
  <%= count_article_summaries %>
</p>
```

The partial we provided to the `settings` attribute gives us an `@settings` instance variable, which will provide the default value of each settings key (assuming we initialized it).

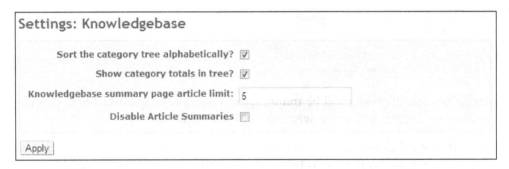

As we can see, the partial renders our content with a predefined heading and an **Apply** button. Also, we didn't have to explicitly define a form as Redmine has provided this functionality for us.

Exposing plugin methods to the settings partial

One of the settings we have is a toggle for whether article summaries should be visible.

As this feature was added after the initial introduction of article summaries, it will be useful to administrators if they could gauge how many people are actually using this feature before they disable it.

First, we'll define a method in `KnowledgebaseSettingsHelper`, which is located at `/path/to/redmine/plugins/redmine_knowlegebase/app/helpers/knowledgebase_settings_helper.rb`.

```
module KnowledgebaseSettingsHelper
  def redmine_knowledgebase_count_article_summaries
    "#{KbArticle.count_article_summaries} of #{KbArticle.count} have
summaries"
  end
end
```

For reference, the `count_article_summaries` method that is cited from the `KbArticle` model is as follows:

```
def self.count_article_summaries
  KbArticle.where("summary is not null and summary <> ''").count
end
```

We'll now update our plugin settings partial to include the summary count. Once this is done, if we try to refresh the page, an error will be displayed as follows:

```
ActionView::Template::Error (undefined local variable or method
 `redmine_knowledgebase_count_article_summaries' for
#<#<Class:0x000000063503f8>:0x000000066c6848>).
```

The issue here is that the context under which our settings partial view runs does not have direct access to our plugin's resources. As a result, none of the custom methods we have in our plugin are available at this point.

In order for Redmine to know what to do with our `redmine_knowedgebase_count_article_summaries` method, we'll need to include our helper as a part of Redmine's `SettingsHelper`.

This can be accomplished by adding the following block to our plugin's initialization file:

```
ActionDispatch::Reloader.to_prepare do
  SettingsHelper.send :include, KnowledgebaseSettingsHelper
end
```

The method of mixing in functionalities is common in Ruby (and Rails). We wrap the call in a `ActionDispatch::Reloader.to_prepare` block (for more information, see `http://api.rubyonrails.org/classes/ActionDispatch/Reloader.html#method-c-to_prepare`) as we want to ensure we don't break any other plugin that can be mixing functionalities into `SettingsHelper`.

Once this is done and our application has been restarted, our plugin settings page will be rendered correctly.

Settings: Knowledgebase

Sort the category tree alphabetically? ☑

Show category totals in tree? ☑

Knowledgebase summary page article limit: 5

Disable Article Summaries ☐ 4 of 8 have summaries

Apply

Note that by injecting our own functionalities into Redmine's SettingsHelper, there's always a chance that we'll override core methods due to identical naming conventions.

As such, it's a good practice to create a separate helper file with only the functions that need to be included in the settings helper and ensure that the methods we include are prefixed such that they stand out as belonging to our plugin.

Accessing our settings

Redmine's Setting model can be used to retrieve the settings values that we've configured.

The Setting model is used internally by Redmine to manage all internal settings. Since the actual values that are being stored are YAML-encoded, they can be more complex than simple strings or integers. The structure of a Setting entry is as follows:

```
Setting(id: integer, name: string, value: text,
    updated_on: datetime)
```

When accessing a plugin settings value, we need to provide the internal name of the setting as well as the key of the specific settings value we want to retrieve. This request takes the following form:

```
Setting['plugin_redmine_knowledgebase'][key]
```

The naming convention used is plugin_#{plugin.id} as this is how Redmine internally manages plugin settings (for more information, see /path/to/redmine/ app/models/setting.rb).

In the previous section, we discussed the disabling of article summaries if the administrator sets the appropriate toggle in our plugin's configuration. The following screenshot is an example of a category list that includes an article with a populated summary:

Title ▲	Created	Updated
Defeating HyperUnpackMe2 With an IDA Processor Module	11 days ago	11 days ago
Memoryze Memory Forensics Tool	11 days ago	11 days ago
The Molecular Virology of Lexotan32: Metamorphism Illustrated	11 days ago	11 days ago
Using IDA Effectively *Up to this tutorial, we learned about the DOS header, the PE header. What remains is the section table. A section table is actually an array of structure immediately following the PE header. The number of the array members is determined by*	24 days ago	24 days ago

Although we've already covered capturing and storing the settings value needed to disable article summaries, in order to apply this setting to our views, we need to include a basic value check. This can be done as follows:

```
<% unless Setting['plugin_redmine_knowledgebase'][:disable_article_
summaries] %>
  <br/>
  <div class="summary">
    <%= article.summary %>
  </div>
<% end %>
```

Now Redmine will check our global settings before trying to display article summaries when browsing a category.

 Although the preceding example illustrates how we can check settings values in our views, the process is identical from within our controllers.

Summary

As our plugins evolve and grow, the number of features will grow as well. Since not all functionality is required in every deployment, allowing administrators to toggle features on and off will make our plugins much more useful for a larger number of installations.

In this chapter, we learned how to take advantage of the built-in settings management functionalities of Redmine and how we can leverage it for our plugins.

In our next chapter, we'll introduce the topic of testing our plugins.

8
Testing Your Plugin

Rails-based projects are structured to allow software tests to be easily incorporated. Most open source projects such as Redmine include tests, and contributors are requested (if not required) to submit tests with their patches. This is especially true for projects written in dynamic languages such as Ruby.

The Redmine core project has excellent test coverage, and if our plugin relies on the core features of Redmine, writing tests is a good way to quickly detect Redmine code changes.

The assumption while going into this chapter is that we are interested in writing tests that can be run in the same environment as the Redmine core project's test suite. Whether we feel that Test Driven Development is beneficial or detrimental to our project and what constitutes a good test are out of the scope of this book as they are extremely subjective topics.

For a good introduction to Test Driven Development as it relates to Rails applications, visit http://andrzejonsoftware.blogspot.ca/2007/05/15-tdd-steps-to-create-rails.html or see the Rails guide to testing applications at http://guides.rubyonrails.org/testing.html.

The following topics will be covered in this chapter:

- Laying out the test directory for your plugin
- Patching the test case classes to allow core and custom fixtures to coexist
- Rake tasks available for running tests
- An overview of the different types of supported tests
- Running tests
- Hooking our plugin into the Travis continuous integration system

Testing infrastructure layout

As we initially used the Redmine plugin generator (see *Chapter 1, Introduction to Redmine Plugins*) when we created our plugin, we should already have a skeletal test directory available for our plugin.

The basic structure of this test folder should be folders named `fixtures`, `functional`, and `unit`, and a `test_helper.rb` file.

```
$ tree test
test
├── fixtures
│   ├── kb_articles.yml
│   └── kb_categories.yml
├── functional
│   ├── articles_controller_test.rb
│   └── categories_controller_test.rb
├── integration
│   ├── accessing_content_test.rb
├── test_helper.rb
└── unit
    ├── article_test.rb
    └── category_test.rb
```

The `test_helper.rb` file that Redmine generates is populated with default configuration, which loads Redmine's main test helper.

Basics of test fixtures

Fixtures are basically just sample data we set up to be used with our tests. They are written as individual entries in YAML files, the files being named after the model they represent. For example, since our article model is stored in a physical `kb_article.rb` file, the associated fixture would be named `kb_articles.yml` and could contain something similar to the following:

```
one:
  id: 1
  category_id: 1
  title: "Sample Article One"
  summary: "Summary of Sample Article One"
  content: "Lorem Ipsum …"
```

Each fixture is named (one, in the preceding example) and is then followed by an indented list of key/value pairs. For a much more detailed dive into fixtures, I would recommend the guide at `http://guides.rubyonrails.org/testing.html#the-low-down-on-fixtures`.

 For more information on Redmine's plugin generators, visit `http://www.redmine.org/projects/redmine/wiki/Plugin_Tutorial#Creating-a-new-Plugin`.

Working around a Redmine testing issue

This book is based on the Redmine 2.3.3 final release, and as such, the scenario described here may not be relevant in future versions of Redmine.

At the time of this writing, if any plugin fixtures are used, the test helper doesn't load them properly. We know our fixtures aren't loaded properly when we add a custom fixture to our test layout and get an error similar to the following on running our tests:

```
# Running tests:

[1/1] ArticlesControllerTest#test_index = 0.02 s
  1) Error:
test_index(ArticlesControllerTest):
Errno::ENOENT: No such file or directory - /path/to/redmine/test/
fixtures/kb_articles.yml
```

Thanks to the tip at `http://www.redmine.org/boards/3/topics/35164?r=3756 5#message-37565`, we can monkey patch `ActionController::TestCase` to work properly for us.

The necessary patch can just be added to our `test_helper.rb`:

```
module Redmine
  module PluginFixturesLoader
    def self.included(base)
      base.class_eval do
        def self.plugin_fixtures(*symbols)
          ActiveRecord::Fixtures.create_fixtures
            (File.dirname(__FILE__) + '/fixtures/', symbols)
        end
      end
    end
  end
end
```

```
unless ActionController::TestCase.included_modules.include?
  (Redmine::PluginFixturesLoader)
  ActionController::TestCase.send :include,
    Redmine::PluginFixturesLoader
End
```

Now that `ActionController::TestCase` is patched, we can include the Redmine core fixtures as well as our plugin's fixtures in our tests.

Note that we'll want to repeat the monkey patch for `ActiveSupport::TestCase` so the same functionality is available when we write our unit tests.

Running tests

Redmine offers some rake tasks to facilitate interacting with a plugin's test suite. These tasks are shown in the following command:

$ rake -T | grep plugins:test

rake redmine:plugins:test

rake redmine:plugins:test:functionals

rake redmine:plugins:test:integration

rake redmine:plugins:test:units

Running any of these rake tasks will run the tests for all installed plugins. In order to limit the tests for our plugin, we need to provide a NAME environment variable.

$ rake redmine:plugins:test:functionals NAME=redmine_knowledgebase

Run options:

 # Running tests:

..

Finished tests in 0.118963s, 16.8119 tests/s, 16.8119 assertions/s.

2 tests, 2 assertions, 0 failures, 0 errors, 0 skips

The rake tasks for running plugin tests are standard `Rake::TestTask` instances (`http://rake.rubyforge.org/classes/Rake/TestTask.html`), so passing options through a `TESTOPTS` environment variable will work the same as if the parameters were provided directly.

```
$ rake redmine:plugins:test:functionals NAME=redmine_knowledgebase
TESTOPTS="-v"
Run options: -v

# Running tests:


ArticlesControllerTest#test_truth = 0.10 s = .
CategoriesControllerTest#test_truth = 0.01 s = .



Finished tests in 0.115128s, 17.3719 tests/s, 17.3719 assertions/s.


2 tests, 2 assertions, 0 failures, 0 errors, 0 skips
```

Writing functional tests

Test cases that target our controller actions are referred to as functional tests. Web requests are received, and the desired response is generally a rendered view.

The Rails guide indicates that some ideal functional test types would be as follows:

- Whether a web request succeeded
- Whether the user was redirected to the correct page
- Whether the user was authenticated
- Whether the proper template was rendered as a response
- Whether the correct message shows in a view

As we'll be using test cases that derive from `ActionController::TestCase` (`http://api.rubyonrails.org/classes/ActionController/TestCase.html`), each functional test case should only test a single controller method.

Here is an example of a functional test for our `ArticlesController`:

```
require File.dirname(__FILE__) + '/../test_helper'
class ArticlesControllerTest < ActionController::TestCase
```

```
    fixtures :projects, :roles, :users
    plugin_fixtures :kb_articles, :enabled_modules

    def setup
      User.current = User.find(1)
      @request.session[:user_id] = 1
      @project = Project.find(1)
    end

    def test_index
      Role.find(1).add_permission! :view_kb_articles
      get :index, :project_id => @project.id

      assert_response :success
      assert_template 'index'
    end
  end
```

A few useful methods have been included in this code, which we'll briefly summarize as follows:

- `fixtures`: The `fixtures` method allows us to include fixtures from Redmine core's test suite (for example, `:issues`, `:roles`, `:users`, `:projects`, and so on)

- `plugin_fixtures`: This is the method we monkey-patched into the various `TestCase` classes so that we could interact with Redmine's fixtures as well as our own custom fixtures

- `@request.session[:user_id] = 1`: If we need to force membership into a project for a specific user, we provide it directly to the session

- `Role.find(1).add_permission! :view_kb_articles`: If we need the current user to have a particular permission in place in order to fulfil a request, we can explicitly add it

Writing integration tests

When we want to test more than one component and examine how they'll function together, or if we want to test the behavior, we write integration tests.

For a more in depth look at Rails integration tests, including what helpers are available, visit `http://guides.rubyonrails.org/testing.html#integration-testing`.

The following is an example of an integration test that accesses a category with an explicitly defined whitelist:

```
require File.dirname(__FILE__) + '/../test_helper'

class AccessingContentTest < ActionController::IntegrationTest
  fixtures :projects, :users
  plugin_fixtures :kb_articles, :kb_categories
  def setup
    @project = Project.find(1)
    @user_1 = User.find(1)
    @user_2 = User.find(2)
  end

  test "access category with an explicit whitelist defined" do
    cat_wl = KbCategory.find(2)
    assert !cat_wl.user_whitelist.blank?, "Category Whitelist expected
to be populated"

    assert !cat_wl.blacklisted?(@user_1), "User 1 is supposed to be
whitelisted"
    assert cat_wl.blacklisted?(@user_2), "User 2 is supposed to not be
whitelisted"
  end
end
```

This is not meant to be an example of how to write a good test, just a very basic integration test.

Writing unit tests

Unit tests within Ruby on Rails applications tend to involve writing tests for models. A good practice is to include tests for all validations, and at least one test per method. Ideally though, tests should be written for anything that could possibly break.

If we were writing the tests first, we would start with something like the following code:

```
require File.dirname(__FILE__) + '/../test_helper'

class CategoryTest < ActiveSupport::TestCase
  plugin_fixtures :kb_categories

  test "should not save category without title" do
```

```
      category = KbCategory.new
      assert !category.save, "Saved the category without a title"
    end
  end
```

If we had yet to configure our model, this test would fail until we added a presence validation to our category model.

Preparing a test database

If this is the first time tests are being run against Redmine, we'll need to first initialize the testing environment.

A test database should first be defined in the path `/path/to/redmine/config/database.yml`, and then the following rake tasks can be run to set up the database:

```
rake db:drop db:create db:migrate redmine:plugins:migrate redmine:load_
default_data RAILS_ENV=test
```

The first command drops the tests database, creates a fresh one, and then runs the Redmine core migrations and all migrations for any installed plugins.

The second command is used to seed the test database with Redmine's default data. For a peek into what constitutes default data, see the contents of `/path/to/redmine/lib/redmine/default_data/loader.rb`.

Once the test database has been initialized, we can use the rake tasks introduced at the beginning of this chapter to run the tests for our plugin.

Note that running the full suite can take a bit of time, so if you're trying to just run a single test case, you can execute it directly.

As an example, if we wanted to run the `ArticlesControllerTest` test case for our knowledgebase plugin, we would execute the following command from the root of our Redmine installation:

```
ruby $(pwd)/plugins/redmine_knowledgebase/test/functional/articles_
controller_test.rb
```

Continuous integration with Travis

Travis CI (`https://travis-ci.org/`) is a hosted continuous integration service for the open source community. It is integrated with GitHub and offers first class support for a number of languages, including Ruby.

Travis is generally meant to run tests against a standalone application, but since we're building plugins for Redmine, we'll need a bit of help in order to bootstrap the process.

Using the samples from `https://github.com/alexbevi/redmine_plugins_travis-ci`, we can configure our plugin to be tested against the latest version of Redmine.

In order to actually integrate our plugin with Travis, the sample files we downloaded from the repository we just mentioned needs to be added to our plugin's root folder, checked into our Git repository, and pushed to GitHub.

More information on the configuration of Travis CI Redmine helpers can be found at `https://github.com/alexbevi/redmine_plugins_travis-ci/blob/master/README.md`.

With the basic tests that we've written for our plugin, once Travis runs, we can check the results on whose website to check whether our tests passed or failed.

The basic layout of a Travis CI test run is broken down into two sections. The first is basic information about which commit triggered the build and the status of the tests run against that build. The second is a build matrix that outlines some information about the test jobs that were run.

If our tests failed, we can drill down further using the build matrix, which lists the various Travis jobs that are associated with the current configuration we've defined for our test environment (visit `http://docs.travis-ci.com/user/build-configuration/#The-Build-Matrix`). The details provided here by Travis should be similar, if not identical, to what we were seeing when running the tests locally.

```
385
386   Finished tests in 0.798992s, 2.5032 tests/s, 2.5032 assertions/s.
387
388     1) Failure:
389   test_should_show_index(ArticlesControllerTest)
      [/home/travis/build/alexbevi/redmine_knowledgebase/workspace/redmine/
      /articles_controller_test.rb:14]:
390   Expected response to be a <:success>, but was <302>
391
392   2 tests, 2 assertions, 1 failures, 0 errors, 0 skips
```

Now that we have our plugin integrated with the Travis CI service, we can update our `README.md` file with a badge that indicates the current status of our plugin's tests.

Wherever we want the badge to appear within the `README.md` file, just add the following sample markdown formatted text:

```
[![Build Status](https://travis-ci.org/<user>/<project>.png)](https://
travis-ci.org/<user>/<project>)
```

The `<user>` and `<project>` values should be replaced by your GitHub username and the project name on GitHub that represents the Redmine plugin we're working on. For our knowledgebase, we will be using `alexbevi/redmine_knowledgebase`.

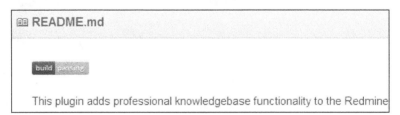

Summary

Test Driven Development and testing in general are very popular among Ruby and Ruby on Rails developers. The fact that any new Rails project that you generate automatically includes basic tests as part of the scaffolding and generators serves as some pretty good reinforcement of that.

This chapter was not meant to serve as an introduction to Test Driven Development or testing or even to try to reinforce the value of writing tests. If the testing tools provided by Rails are not suitable to our needs, there are numerous testing frameworks available that can be used instead. There are also a myriad breakdowns of what types of tests should be written for what types of scenarios and under what circumstances.

Redmine has very good code coverage and provides a lot of excellent examples of the basic test types in its own `test/` directory. Our tests in this chapter were meant to be examples of how to tie plugin testing into Redmine's testing infrastructure and how Redmine test assets could be accessed therein.

In our final chapter, we'll be gaining some insight into the process of releasing our plugin to the Redmine community as well as some tips to encourage community participation.

Releasing Your Plugin

Congratulations! You've now built a plugin that can be used to add value to any Redmine deployment. There is, however, one last step in the process: release management.

This isn't really an authorship step, and as such is being included as an appendix. This is also not meant to be taken as the only way a plugin can be released, but a set of suggestions that will help give you exposure within the Redmine community. The following topics will be covered in this appendix:

- Getting your source code online
- Writing about your releases
- Publishing your plugin to Redmine's plugin directory
- Promoting your plugin on Redmine's forums

Managing your plugin's source code

The assumption being made is that you're planning on releasing your plugin's source code under an open source license. If you're working on a proprietary plugin, please disregard this section.

Depending on what source control tools you're using, there are different communities available online that offer free hosting of source code for public projects:

- Git (http://git-scm.com)
    - ° GitHub (https://github.com)
    - ° Gitorious (https://gitorious.org)

- Subversion (http://subversion.apache.org)
    - ° Google Code (https://code.google.com)
    - ° SourceForge (http://sourceforge.net)

- Mercurial (`http://mercurial.selenic.com`)
  - Bitbucket (`https://bitbucket.org`)
  - Codeplex (`http://www.codeplex.com`)

This list is not meant to be an exhaustive one; it's meant only to serve as links to some of the most popular hosting solutions based on the source control tool you choose. The majority of these sites actually host more than one source control tool, so you've got options!

We will be using Git and GitHub for our examples, as this combo is quite popular among Redmine developers, as well as the Ruby community as a whole.

Depending on your level of experience with Git, you may want to read `https://help.github.com/articles/set-up-git` first, as this covers most of what is required in order to get started with Git. Continuing with the GitHub help pages will also assist with getting a repository configured, checking your code in, and pushing your code to GitHub for the world to see. The following is a screenshot of the Redmine knowledgebase GitHub page:

Now that our plugin is online and available, we'll want to ensure that we have **Issues management** enabled. This feature allows users and other developers to provide feedback and bug reports.

If you decide not to use GitHub, most (if not all) other available source management sites will provide some form of issue tracking feature.

Starting a blog

Now that our source has been published, we should write about why we created this plugin in the first place.

Actually, starting a blog is a bit out of the scope for this book, but if you're new to this process I would recommend **GitHub Pages** (`http://pages.github.com`), **WordPress** (`http://wordpress.com`), or **Blogger** (`http://www.blogger.com`).

Whether the goal was to solve a particular problem at work, fulfill some edge case we identified, or just scratch an itch, providing a bit of extra information about our motivation may help to encourage some users to take our plugin for a spin.

Once we begin to revise our plugin and add new features, the blog can also be used to announce new versions and include change log information.

A link to the blog can also be included within our plugin's initialization section as the `author_url` value (see *Chapter 1, Introduction to Redmine Plugins* for more information).

Publishing your plugin on redmine.org

Once our source control needs have been met and our introductory site has been established, we can introduce our plugin to the Redmine community at `http://www.redmine.org/plugins/`.

Plugins Directory   ⊙ Register a new plugin

Here you can browse and search Redmine plugins. Plugin developers can register their own plugins using their redmine.org account. General information about Redmine plugins and how to install them into your Redmine can be found at Plugins.

Create an account and navigate to the plugin directory at `http://www.redmine.org/plugins`. From the plugin management screen, we can register our new plugin via the **Register a new plugin** link.

To register our plugin, we need to provide some basic information such as the plugin name, identifier, description, home page, code repository, a thumbnail, and any additional installation notes. Next, we'll have to provide details about the current version that we've just released:

The **Redmine compatibility** section is a series of checkboxes that we set to indicate which version(s) of Redmine our plugin is known to work with.

The **Files** section can be used to attach an archive of this version of the plugin, assuming it doesn't exceed the maximum file size of 500 KB. If this is the case, we will have to host the file elsewhere and link to it in the **Release Notes** section, which is available after we publish our plugin or any time we add a new version.

Announcing your plugin on redmine.org

With our initial release available within Redmine's plugin directory, we'll want to make an announcement in the Redmine forums as well advertise our release.

Navigate to `http://www.redmine.org/projects/redmine/boards`, select the **Plugins** board, and then click on **New message**.

The subject should be kept brief and mention the name of the plugin listed (possibly as we listed it in our `init.rb` file under the `name` attribute).

The actual contents of this first post should give a brief introduction of what the plugin does, as well as provide links to the plugin in the plugin directory on GitHub (or whatever source control system we've selected):

Redirect issue with Redmine Meetings	Donald Slagle	2013-01-02 23:54	1	Added by Richard Rauch about 1 month ago RE: Redirect issue with Redmine Meetings
Knowledgebase Plugin	Alex Bevilacqua	2010-02-22 16:54	123	Added by Ionut moraru about 1 month ago RE: Knowledgebase Plugin
ckeditor : paste from excel	Gurvan Le Dromaguet	2013-09-26 08:43	0	

If you composed a particularly clean and concise blog post introducing the plugin, you could simply copy and paste the contents as the introductory forum post.

Initially, this post will likely be the primary communication channel for feedback for your plugin, so make sure you keep it "watched" and respond to the community in a timely fashion.

Summary

Our plugin is now out in the wild and we're quickly gathering a devoted user base. It is important to take ownership of our plugin and review the issue reports, feature requests, e-mails, forum posts, and whatever other feedback the community may provide.

In this appendix, we covered some basic steps that can be taken in order to publish our plugin using features that Redmine (http://www.redmine.org) makes available, as well as some basic source control services that are freely available.

This concludes our journey into Redmine plugin extension and development. I hope this guide has answered most of your questions regarding the topics we've covered. If not, there is a vast community available online at http://www.redmine.org, and a multitude of projects in various stages of completion hosted at https://github. com that can be used to answer questions or draw inspiration.

Cheers and happy coding!

Index

M

management
  configuring 71, 72
Mercurial
  URL 90
model hooks 25, 26
models
  access restrictions 33
  preparing 43, 44, 63
  preparing, to be searched 54, 55
  registering 63, 64
model, view, and controller (MVC) 7

N

new plugin
  controllers, generating 11, 12
  custom gemsets, using in 10
  generating 8, 10
  models, generating 11

P

permissions
  about 29-31
  custom permissions, declaring 31-33
plugin
  announcing, on redmine.org 92
  publishing, on redmine.org 91, 92
  registering 53, 54
  score card, managing 89, 90
plugin_fixtures method 82
plugin methods
  exposing, to settings partial 72, 73
project_module block 18

R

Rails-based projects 77
Rails Engines plugin 10
Redmine
  about 7, 21
  permissions system 29
  testing issue 79, 80
Redmine compatibility section 92
Redmine core project 77

redmine.org
  plugin, announcing on 92
  plugin, publishing on 91, 92
redmine_plugin generator 9
render_on helper method 23
Rubygems
  URL 36
Ruby on Rails framework 7
Ruby on Rails migrations
  URL 37

S

sample plugin 7
search
  article content, including 58
search options
  configuring 55, 56
search results
  filtering, custom permissions used 57, 58
Semantic Versioning 14
settings management
  enabling 70, 71
settings model
  accessing 74, 75
Sourceforge
  URL 89
Subversion
  URL 89

T

tests
  database, preparing 84
  fixtures 78, 79
  functional tests, writing 81, 82
  integration tests, writing 82, 83
  running 80, 81
  unit tests, writing 83, 84
Travis
  continuous integration with 84-86

U

unit tests
  writing 83, 84
user whitelists
  managing 37-39

V

view hooks 22, 23
view partial
  creating 27
views
  access restrictions 33, 35
  attachments, enabling 45, 46

W

whitelist
  enforcing 39, 40
WordPress
  URL 90

Thank you for buying
Redmine Plugin Extension and Development

About Packt Publishing

Packt, pronounced 'packed', published its first book "*Mastering phpMyAdmin for Effective MySQL Management*" in April 2004 and subsequently continued to specialize in publishing highly focused books on specific technologies and solutions.

Our books and publications share the experiences of your fellow IT professionals in adapting and customizing today's systems, applications, and frameworks. Our solution based books give you the knowledge and power to customize the software and technologies you're using to get the job done. Packt books are more specific and less general than the IT books you have seen in the past. Our unique business model allows us to bring you more focused information, giving you more of what you need to know, and less of what you don't.

Packt is a modern, yet unique publishing company, which focuses on producing quality, cutting-edge books for communities of developers, administrators, and newbies alike. For more information, please visit our website: www.packtpub.com.

About Packt Open Source

In 2010, Packt launched two new brands, Packt Open Source and Packt Enterprise, in order to continue its focus on specialization. This book is part of the Packt Open Source brand, home to books published on software built around Open Source licences, and offering information to anybody from advanced developers to budding web designers. The Open Source brand also runs Packt's Open Source Royalty Scheme, by which Packt gives a royalty to each Open Source project about whose software a book is sold.

Writing for Packt

We welcome all inquiries from people who are interested in authoring. Book proposals should be sent to author@packtpub.com. If your book idea is still at an early stage and you would like to discuss it first before writing a formal book proposal, contact us; one of our commissioning editors will get in touch with you.

We're not just looking for published authors; if you have strong technical skills but no writing experience, our experienced editors can help you develop a writing career, or simply get some additional reward for your expertise.

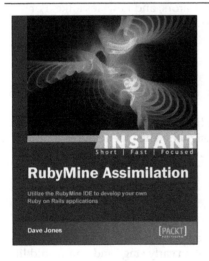

RubyMotion iOS Development Essentials

ISBN: 978-1-84969-522-0   Paperback: 262 pages

Create apps that utilize iOS device capabilities without learning Objective-C

1. Get your iOS apps ready faster with RubyMotion.

2. Use iOS device capabilities such as GPS, camera, multitouch, and many more in your apps.

3. Learn how to test your apps and launch them on the AppStore.

4. Use Xcode with RubyMotion and extend your RubyMotion apps with Gems.

Ext JS 4 Plugin and Extension Development

ISBN: 978-1-78216-372-5   Paperback: 116 pages

A hands-on development of several Ext JS plugins and extensions

1. Easy-to-follow examples on Ext JS plugins and extensions.

2. Step-by-step instructions on developing Ext JS plugins and extensions.

3. Provides a walkthrough of several useful Ext JS libraries and communities.

Please check **www.PacktPub.com** for information on our titles